Advance praise for *The*

"In his novels and short stories, Randall Kenan has proved a master of place making. In *The Carolina Table*, he renders place through food, framing North Carolina in 'ballads to hunger' and 'hymns of satiation.' This choir sings of cheese puffs straight from the bag and pollo a la brasa straight from Peru, while connecting the Fertile Crescent of the Middle East and the Piedmont of North Carolina. Smart, inclusive, generous, and, at times, evocatively random, *The Carolina Table* sets a national standard for food writing collections."

—John T Edge, author of *The Potlikker Papers: A Food History of the Modern South*

"Read *The Carolina Table* and you pull up your chair to the best groaning boards in the state. Randall Kenan's choices are acute, delicious, and big-hearted. I love the family lore, the discourse on butter beans, the recipe for grape hull pie, free use of the word 'fatback,' and the elements of cleaning crab—beer, a hose, mosquitos. Most of all, I love the humor and the quirky voices of my Southern brethren."

—Frances Mayes, author of *Under the Tuscan Sun* and most recently *Under Magnolia: A Southern Memoir*

"If it's true that by knowing what we eat, we know who we are, then *The Carolina Table* serves us up a cultural treasury of Southern food and how to cook it, eat it and pass it down through generations. This is our Anatomy of the Culinary. Tar Heel essayists, journalists, novelists, poets, chef and critics evocatively fill the pages of *The Table* with reminiscences particular to them but resonate for all: how food and the inheritance of recipes construct our holiday rituals, our family reunions, our shared memories. From the region's beloved classics, like shrimp and grits, pecan pie, barbecue, and fried chicken, from the traditional products of its fisheries and farms and dairies (the crab, pork, greens and beans, and buttermilk), to today's modern local celebrity chefs and restaurants, *The Carolina Table* sets out an absolute banquet of a book. Have a seat and welcome to the feast."

—Michael Malone, author of *Handling Sin* and *Four Corners of the Sky*

☀ THE CAROLINA TABLE ☀

THE CAROLINA TABLE

North Carolina Writers on Food

RANDALL KENAN

EDITOR

publishers

The Carolina Table: North Carolina Writers on Food
Editor Randall Kenan
© Eno Publishers 2016

Eno Publishers
P.O. Box 158
Hillsborough, North Carolina 27278
www.enopublishers.org

ISBN: 978-0-9973144-0-3
Library of Congress Control Number: 2016950806
First edition, second printing

❋ ❋ ❋

Cover photograph of the kitchen of April McGregor
(Farmer's Daughter) in Hillsborough, North Carolina, by Chris Fowler
Design and production by Copperline Book Services,
Hillsborough, North Carolina

Eno Publishers wishes to thank the Orange
County Arts Commission for its generous
support in helping to fund *The Carolina Table*.

ORANGE COUNTY ARTS
COMMISSION

☀ EDITOR'S ACKNOWLEDGMENTS ☀

I WOULD LIKE to thank each of our contributors for answering the call despite a world of distractions. A big thanks to Marcie Cohen Ferris, Kelly Alexander, and John T. Edge for encouraging my spasmodic forays into writing about the world of food. And a note of thanks to folks at Eno Publishers—particularly to Laura Lacy and Sophie Shaw—and to Elizabeth Woodman for seducing me with this particular honey pot, which was yummy yummy for my tummy.

—*Randall Kenan*

CONTENTS

Carolina Flavor

Adventures in Eating

Traditions

Afterword

☀ HOME IN MIND ☀

there are stains on my grandmother's apron
leavings of gravies & crookneck yellow squash,
turkey dressing blended by hand, molasses with fatback
to be sopped, memories tucked in its yellowing folds

there are things that make us remember
the peppery vinegar of Down-East barbeque,
of collard greens, sugared beets, sweet-tasseled corn
grown in dirt tinged with that Cackalacky red-clay

there are kitchens with tins of drippings on the stove,
leavings to be ladled into stews & cracklin' bread
& apple-jacks fried in the black cast-iron pan
that my mother handed down to me

there are things that only pot likker can cure &
times when what actually matters can be spooned
on to a plate—the savories & the sweetest of things—
that simply taste like my North Carolina home

—*Sheila Smith McKoy*

☀ THE CAROLINA TABLE ☀

INTRODUCTION

The Rooster, the Rattlesnake, and the Hydrangea Bush

☀ RANDALL KENAN ☀

WHEN I WAS a little bitty boy, no more than four, I carried on a feud with a rooster. This rooster had no name, nor was it a colorful bird. Dun white it was, with a set of vivid red wattles which provoked within me a rather reptilian revulsion. I would chase the rooster, and in turn, the rooster, letting out a chanticleer squawk, would chase me.

My childhood was not exactly idyllic, but I wouldn't trade it for Mark Zuckerberg's billions. Sustenance surrounded us, demanding industry and thrift. We might have been poor but we were never hungry. My cousin Norman and his wife, Miss Alice, lived directly across the dirt road from our house. I remember every divot and rise and slope of their emerald front yard where I'd run back and forth with this maniacal bird. I remember the great and ancient oak tree at the very edge, too big to climb, with its gnarled above-the-earth roots straight out of a Grimm brothers' fairy story. I remember the barn and pigpen to the east and the orchard to the west. It seems in those days every farmer with his own land had an orchard of some design. Cousin Norman's contained: a peach tree; a number of pear trees; and a multitude of horse apple trees, the little green apples essential to making the tartest, most magical apple pies over which a boy might dream and drool; tall and productive walnut trees; pecan trees aplenty. Cousin Norman's farm sat on a bend of a branch or creek that snaked off and to the Northeast Cape Fear River. A grape arbor grew mighty close to the water. In autumn that grape arbor produced the plumpest, sweetest, purplest scuppernongs known to man or beast. Grapes weren't the only thing that brackish branch produced.

The truth is I remember this day largely the way one remembers a Polaroid picture one took in haste. It became one of those stories told and retold so often the tellings are mixed with what actually happened. Unbidden, a cousin recounted this story to me at our last family reunion. I know he was in New Jersey at the time. Nonetheless, this much is true:

Cousin Norman and Miss Alice were sitting on their high concrete front porch. Miss Alice liked to dip snuff, and she would spit on occasion with great accuracy off that porch, often into this vast hydrangea bush to the east of the porch. Front-yard hydrangea bushes are not uncommon, even something of a standard in the South. But I recollect these bushes, like that oak tree, to have been of legendary proportion, not unlike those monstrous cabbages one only sees at the state fair. As soon as I walked into their yard, the rooster came flying at me, its powerful thighs pumping, its talons clawing at the earth. Had I eaten one too many of his children?

Not to be undone, I puffed up my chest, Tarzan-like, and rushed the feathery juggernaut, causing it to turn-tail and make a mad dash for the hydrangea bush.

Fairly swiftly a mighty ruckus ensued. The great bush commenced to shimmy and shake, its green leaves to tremble earthquake-like (though at age four, the idea of an earthquake would have been as foreign to me as a credit default swap). The rooster ejected itself from the bush rather like a white cannonball and made a beeline toward the smokehouse. The hydrangea bush continued to shake and rattle. At this stage both Cousin Norman and Miss Alice were standing, agog. Indeed, Miss Alice was hollering. Foolishly I moved closer to investigate. She was hollering at me to get away. Cousin Norman had gone into the house, and would return soon with a shotgun. What I could see, only in flashes, was a diamondback rattlesnake, coiling itself round and round the base of the hydrangea bush, causing its entirety to shake in this indecent fashion.

I did not see Cousin Norman dispatch the reptile, for I had made my greatest imitation of a chicken I would make in my brief life.

* * *

THIS WAS IN rural Duplin County, North Carolina, once the epicenter of tobacco, currently the epicenter of pigs and poultry. My home, my world, was always edible. A moveable feast.

* * *

ONE OF MY earliest memories is the death of Great-Uncle Redden when I was three. We were out grading flue-cured tobacco, and he succumbed to a blood clot on the porch of a house used to prepare the cooked brightleaf and pack it up into bails wrapped and secured by large burlap canvasses. Grading—separating quality from trash, smoothing them for market, one by one—was a tedious job, and largely done by women.

I don't remember the specific women there that day, though I suspect I do, for I remember their faces surrounding my Great-Aunt Mary (whom I called Mama, the woman who raised me). What immediately followed would be something I'd witness for the rest of my growing up: People showing up heavy-laden with food to the homes of the recently deceased. Hams, fried chicken, oven-baked barbecue chicken, pork chops smothered in gravy, dirty rice, Spanish rice, potato salad galore, slaw, sweet potato casseroles, candied yams, hushpuppies, cornbread, soup, chopped pork barbecue, collard greens, pound cake, chocolate cake, coconut cake, pineapple cake, red velvet cake, sweet potato pie, lemon meringue pie: My mother's lemon meringue pie was both performance art and sorcery—it enchanted everyone who looked upon it and who tasted it.

The idea here of course being that the immediate family would not have to think about cooking or where to find food. Everything was taken care of. There is a lovely passage in one of the early editions of Emily Post's *Etiquette*. She instructs us not to ask the bereaved if they would like something to eat, rather we should make a warm bowl of broth and put it in the bereaved hands with a spoon.

("We gather with food because food is the ultimate and final expression of how we love and the culture of our community. . . . The laying out of the dead and the laying out of the food pull me closer and closer to that vortex of all things familiar and comfortable." See Jaki Shelton Green's food story, "Singing Tables.")

In the end we are talking about expressions of love, not the sentimental, Hallmark-card version, but material, immediate, unambiguous demonstrations that you care, that you are there. It is practical, it is flavorful, and it is real.

When you grow up in a small rural community, it seems everyone is related to everyone, somebody is somebody else's cousin. Everyone knows everybody else. It seems like a lot of people are dying because you are acutely aware of every death—you probably ate Sunday supper with that person at one point, you probably visited their sick bed, went to school with them, certainly went to church with them.

* * *

IT IS DIFFICULT to look back on these dire gatherings without just a little mirth. Despite the somber setting, there was still a party-like atmosphere about the proceedings. Usually relatives would come from far and wide (New York, Washington, Detroit), a sense of homecoming like a family reunion. Or as Lyle Lovett once sang:

> I went to a funeral,
> and Lord it made me happy.
> Seeing all those people
> That I ain't seen
> since the last time
> Somebody died.

Here's the Coca-Cola, here's the lemonade, here's the sweet ice tea, here's the fruit punch, here's Uncle Roma's mason jar full of bootleg moonshine, or a jug of homemade scuppernong wine. Here it is because we are all human. And as it says in the Good Book, "Man shall not live by bread alone."

*   *   *

CERTAIN OF US sons and daughters of the South have a chip on our shoulders about stereotypes regarding the American South. Portrayals, clichés, misconceptions about what it means to be a Southerner in the twenty-first century in North Carolina can be worrisome at best. Friends of mine I presume to be more secure than I don't give a flying rooster what people in New York or Los Angeles or Paris, France, think of them, and they ask me, "Why do you care? You have no investment in this North vs. South silliness." Nonetheless some of us still smart as if by hornet bite at the residue of the implication that *Southern* means backward, ill-educated, lazy, superstitious, unhygienic, and dumb. But I suspect, at bottom, my aloof friends do care, but just don't care to talk about it.

One thing I've learned as an adult is that not all super-intelligent people are necessarily reflective about themselves and about the world.

Foodways are too often lumped in with all the other overarching folksy, old-fashioned, technophobic, churchified, photocopies of Mayberry and The General Lee. Things get even more complicated when the element or icon in question holds a special place for the Southerner. (Andy Griffith, grits, okra.) Yes, many of us adore fried chicken; yes, a great many of us have strong feelings about barbecue, and sweet ice tea. That does not mean everything we eat is fried (from turkey to Milky Way bars to butter—though some do—and it is true that in my mother's home town, Rose Hill, you can find the world's largest frying pan, used each year to fry a record-breaking amount of chicken during the Poultry Jubilee), or that vegetables are of little import and are meant to be boiled into shameful, tasteless mush, if not fried. Historical nuance is rare in these too-frequent caricatures. A great many Southerners aid and abet these visions of the Old North State and its environs. So much so that sometimes railing against stereotypes feels quixotic at best; futile even on a good day. Nonetheless, we find ourselves like William Faulkner's young

Quentin Compson having to state the affirmative with a denial. "I don't hate it. . . . I don't. I don't! . . . I don't hate it! I don't."

*　*　*

WHY FOOD?

So let me tell about the South. Let me tell what do they do there. How do they live there. Why do they.

The serious study of food and foodways in the academy is still a relatively young discipline, and is still having a hard time gaining the respect it deserves (see Marcie Ferris's "The Big Book of North Carolina Foodways," this book's Afterword). Eating is something we must do in order to live. I know people who think of food as merely fuel for their body. Something to stave off hunger. To them thinking overmuch—and surely writing—about food is pure decadence, the stuff of gluttony and the idle well-off. For so long gastronomy (the technical name for food writing) was the province of the elitist gourmands with money to burn and no concern for their health or waistline. In conjunction with those who actively disrespect food writing and the study of foodways are those who don't think of food at all, beyond chomping down on a Quarter Pounder, finding the cheapest Chinese buffet lunch, or scarfing down Buffalo wings and fries while watching the NCAA tournaments.

Speaking of fancy French words, the guy who came up with the idea of a dedicated discipline to writing about food and who gave us the word *gastronomy* was a Frenchman named Jean Anthelme Brillat-Savarin (1755–1826). His masterwork, *The Physiology of Taste*, is often quoted, in particular this line: "Tell me what you eat and I will tell you what you are." There, truly, is the rub.

History, geography, business, culture, science, demography, labor, narrative, myth, and folklore, even music, all intersect in the world of food. Can there be a North Carolina without sweet potatoes, blueberries, and cucumbers? (Do most North Carolinians know that our state produces more sweet potatoes than any other state? This represents 50 percent of the United States' supply. Or that our still youngish wine industry brings in over $1 billion a year; but more, that our industry grew on the backs of the muscadine, which is one of the few grapes indigenous to North America and prolific in North Carolina.) These connections are neither vague nor frivolous, but central to our state's character and the character of its people, even those who sincerely believe their lives are untouched by food they don't put in their mouths. Very serious stories like the crisis among black farmers losing their farms, the ecological damage caused by industrial hog farms, and food insecurity in Southern urban areas (ironically), all embrace economics, the environment, race, social justice, health, and so much more.

This is the story of the Tar Heel state through food.

* * *

I AM SO proud and grateful to each of the writers who have contributed to *The Carolina Table,* for they each give us a very real and powerful glimpse into a true North Carolina. They tell about the South. They approach it largely, firstly, in a personal way—we see, we smell, we hear, but most importantly, we taste North Carolina through the pens of these talented folk. To me these are food songs, ballads to hunger, hymns of satiation, odes to gustatory joy; but also ditties to disaster, and madrigals of misunderstanding. The generous nature of these writers serves up such a complex portrait of our state, our ways, and our people with which few can argue against.

Whether it's novelist and Clinton native Michael Parker's remembrances of his food-writing mother, no great fan of cooking, much to her family's despair; or Jacksonville poet and Haiku-master Lenard Moore's snapshot of his Down East family through food ("the silver pan piled with fish in it, smelling of the sea on the long, wooden table in the backyard"); or Elizabeth Engelhardt's paternal olfactory misfortunes—in the end these stories are about the people, their complexity, their quirks, their tastes, their priorities, their communities. All so wonderfully captured in Nancie McDermott's recollections of her family reunions and what they ate there. Though the predominant presences—English, Scots-Irish, African, and Lumbee/Cherokee—are loud and strong in this early part of the twenty-first century, many other voices are calling, have called North Carolina home. Richard Chess evokes Southern Jewry in his piece about food and the Friday night Shabbat; Paul Cuadros introduces us to a new style of cooked chicken imported from Peru; newcomers like Sophia Woo, and her powerfully innovative Raleigh food truck, Pho Nomenal Dumpling Truck, breathe new air into our diet; Diya Abdo's moving testimony about caring for Syrian refugees in Guilford County speaks to the universality of food's power to comfort and heal; as does the poetic essay by Zelda Lockhart from the Piedmont, but whose African American roots mirror my Down East roots so fittingly, calling up image to image my earliest, dearest, and most true North Carolina memories.

Not only do we cry, but we also laugh. Celia Rivenbark's recollections of working in a beloved Down East barbecue restaurant—family style, as down home as "down home" gets—captures not only her wry humor, but is indicative of where that trademark humor came from. Jill McCorkle offers memories of a cake deeply embedded in her Lumberton family. Our geography is famously wide: John McElwee writes about the shad festival in coastal Jamestown; Michael McFee revisits a largely forgotten writer and editor for the Asheville *Citizen-Times* who for forty-two years captured mountain cuisine and foodways with the runaway lyricism of a Thomas Wolfe. "Peppermint mornings," indeed. Though Charlotte and the Piedmont stuff this *omnium gatherum* about N.C. food, we feel that our toes are digging into the beach sand while our heads are peering over Mt. Mitchell.

We contain multitudes.

*　　*　　*

THERE IS A place in Atlanta I insist on visiting every time I'm in town. The Dekalb Farmers Market. Few places—especially in the American South—bring together so many cultures, so many foods, so many people, from around the globe. I like going there not just for the grains from Ethiopia, the nuts from Israel, the fruits from India and Malaysia, the fish from Europe, or the vegetables from Venezuela—foods you won't be finding at the local Food Lion or the Harris Teeter—but also to see the people, this polyglot, multi-ethnic, multicolored parade of humanity coming together over one thing: food. People from warring backgrounds, people who are sworn enemies, gather together peacefully in a foreign land. Israelis and Egyptians, the Japanese and the Korean. To me this is a more practical United Nations, and effectively so. This represents the power of food, more than to stop hunger, more than to feed gluttony, more than sales and business.

Of course I recognize that this is a naive daydream of a world-besotted professional dreamer. I know that food cannot accomplish what politics, mighty armies, crushing economies, and slick science can achieve. Though I do know that all generals and senators eat, as do business moguls and geneticists.

Nowadays places like Carrboro and Durham and Raleigh and Charlotte and Asheville and Wilmington are becoming more like the Dekalb Farmers Market. It is a gradual thing. Incremental. And, to be sure, some of my fellow North Carolinians harbor a lot of anxiety over that change. What will happen to the old ways? they mutter. They see falafels as a threat; cactus pads as enemy combatants; sea cucumber as an arch invader. I hasten to remind them that in London and in Toronto, two of the world's most multicultural cities, you can still easily get spotted dick, Welsh rarebit, and poutine. Barbecue and fried chicken are not going away anytime soon. (Today salsa outsells tomato catsup in every state in the Union. Yet the Constitution still stands. Meanwhile taco trucks are blossoming all over out state like cherry blossoms in Washington, DC, in April. And we're the better for it.)

Some folk see the American South as a bug trapped in amber; others see the South as an integral part of the great American Experiment—

still aspiring to get it right, to make it better; an ongoing thing—rich with contributions, opportunities, and possibilities.

I do dream and wonder about our state's culinary future. What will newcomers bring and support, what of our past will they adopt, what blends and hybrids might occur, what new crops will we begin to grow, what new uses might we discover for sweet potatoes and tobacco plants and pine needles and the humble butter bean?

SOMEONE'S IN THE KITCHEN

Singing Tables

✳ JAKI SHELTON GREEN ✳

I'M NEVER COOKING alone, even at my most solitary moments. I am surrounded by generations of cooks, their wisdom, their laughter, and their flawed and perfect recipes lifting my hands and heart, savoring each ingredient as I realize that each ingredient represents all the joys, sorrows, healing, and restoration of my life's journey. These unseen hands hold me in passionate surrender to generosity, as family and friends gather at my table reminding me that food creates community, holds my sense of identity, and conjures sensory surprises over and over again. The ghosts of other tables, other kitchens, remind me that we are all just ingredients and what matters is the grace with which I cook the meal.

My food odyssey is a soundtrack remix like the texture of an autobiography offering a throwback to prayer-song, dance, birth, death, sex, and rock and roll. The backyard chicken coops, vegetable gardens, and mini-orchards are long gone, like my elders and the neighborhood of my childhood. What remains is me . . . the brown woman-child writing down the sizzle of cast-iron skillets, the bold of the beet, the hot of the pepper pot, the earthiness of walnuts, and the bitter of arugula.

Food helps me to express my past and present. Food helps me to create communal ties and honor my ancestral roots.

> Blessed assurance, Jesus is mine!
> Oh, what a foretaste of glory divine!

Heir of salvation, purchase of God,
Born of his Spirit, washed in his blood.
—*Frances Crosby*

My grandmother, Eva White Tate, hosted the Ora Shanklin African Methodist Episcopal Missionary meetings that gathered monthly on first Monday evenings during the springs and summers of my youth. An agenda of devotions, song, prayer, and scripture segued into Old and New Business, projects to raise money for their many charitable activities, missionary dues, and a "love offering" for the sick. My grandmother, mother, and aunts raced around all day preparing food and setting an elegant table for the elaborately coiffed church ladies in their flawless pristine summer linen, pastels, crepe de chine, patent leather, and sexy sling-backs that made ticky-tacky squeals across the glistening, freshly waxed wood floor.

This monthly soirée featured milk-glass vases holding peony globes and arrangements of snapdragons, Queen Anne's lace, and foxgloves strategically placed on the crisp white linen tablecloth adorning the antique oak dining table, monogrammed linen napkins, and the heirloom silverware that was left to my tiny hands to polish on a regular basis. I was impressed that the deviled eggs required their own unique platter, designed especially for deviled eggs. Mounds of homemade chicken salad garnished with apples, pecans, and grapes, potato salad, pear walnut salad, canapés of cucumber dill cream cheese, pimento cheese, stuffed olives, and perfectly browned chicken legs were presented on sparkling crystal and carnival glass serving platters.

The inlaid glass sideboard was majestic with a centerpiece of magnolia, camellia, and gardenia blossoms fresh-cut from my grandmother's flower garden, and cut-glass pedestals of scrumptious coconut cake, frosted lemon pound petit fours, homemade mints (pink, green, yellow), fresh strawberries, chocolate-covered peanuts, and my grandmother's famous secret-recipe egg custard. Pitchers of brewed mint tea and punch bowls bearing icy rainbow sherbet framed both sides of the dessert display, waiting to be admired and devoured by the white-gloved missionaries.

This pageantry of memory continues to feed my upper crust soul. This pageantry was the backdrop for all the whispered gossips and secrets of uppity church women in between "a piece of this and a little dab of that."

> Summertime, and the livin' is easy,
> Fish are jumpin' and the cotton is high,
> Oh, your daddy's rich and your ma is good looking,
> So hush little baby, don't you cry.
> —*Dubose Heyward*

The smell of coffee brewing, bacon frying, and hot biscuits browning was the only summer alarm clock in our house. The first few weeks of school vacation my brother and I spent lazy days playing between our house and Aunt Alice's house or hanging out at Uncle Ervin's service station pretending to be proprietors behind the counter, taking money for gas, candy, milk, bread, but never the cigarettes. That fun would be interrupted when "the garden came in" with lima beans, snap beans, wax beans, okra, peas, squash, cucumbers, tomatoes, cantaloupe, cabbage, lettuce, watermelon, and corn. The litany from porch to porch throughout the neighborhood addressed to our bored little brown bodies was "shut up whining . . . your little bellies will be glad to get this food come winter time. Don't put those hulls in that bowl." So we pouted in between snapping, shucking, peeling, and rinsing so the grown folks could can, freeze, stew, and preserve.

These were the summers when our "Up South" Northern kinfolks took a notion to jump in a car or hop a bus or train and show up unannounced usually with five or six children in tow. Our family had abundant land and food so this uncouth behavior never daunted my mom, grandmother, and aunts. They knew how to "hold their mouths right" and bring forth their best masks of civility, so refined that no one ever read their furious annoyance hidden beneath the labor of love. For two or three weeks, they laid out daily breakfast, lunch, and supper smorgasbords of cured smoked ham and red-eye gravy, scrambled cheese eggs, grits, salmon croquettes, biscuits, bacon, sausage, homemade peach, strawberry, blackberry, pear jelly and preserves, stewed apples, potato cakes, cinnamon rolls, and toast. The *guests* would feast and then retreat to the front porch, the yard, the television, or return to bed to sleep away their city blues.

With the guests out of the way, the women folks washed dishes, swept crumbs, cleared the table, and talked in hushed ridicule and dismay about their hungry citified relatives. After they caught their breath and a few of the leftover table scraps, they started the operation for lunch or "just a little something to tide them over" which was usually homemade egg, tuna, or chicken salad, the optional ham and cheese sandwich, tossed salad, chilled watermelon and cantaloupe, ice tea and fresh lemonade, all served outside on the porch.

Fried chicken, fried fish, turnip salad, chicken and dumplings, stewed tomatoes, potato salad, rice pudding, fried okra and squash, pound cake, apple pie, and yeast rolls made the "Up South" folks remember where home really was. They never suspected by our good manners how their unannounced visits interrupted our summer explorations, building camps and forts in the woods, fishing, skinny-dipping, catching tadpoles, making June-bug whistles, chasing lightning bugs, and baking mud-pies all day in the sun.

> If you want to know
> Where I'm going
> Where I'm going, soon
> If anybody ask you
> Where I'm going
> Where I'm going soon
> I'm going up yonder
> I'm going up yonder
> To be with my Lord.
> —*Tremaine Hawkins*

Death often disrupts my family and community. We gather with food because food is the ultimate and final expression of how we love, and the culture of our community. Feasting with the dead even now and in my past continues to provide me a way to reconnect and maintain connections with my ancestors and my daughter. My family and extended tribes have never needed a copy of *Being Dead Is No Excuse: The Official Southern Ladies Guide to Hosting the Perfect Funeral.* It's in our blood . . . we know what we know about the power of fried gizzards, leftover meat loaf, turkey necks, fried croakers, okra gumbo, and moonshine.

The laying out of the dead and the laying out of the food pull me closer and closer to that vortex of all things familiar and comfortable. These are forever images imbedded in my mind's rolling video screen of the deaths of my father, grandmother, aunts, uncles, cousins, and my daughter.

When my precious daughter, Imani, died, people came with their stories of her life neatly folded in the corners of picnic baskets. They delivered their stories of her whimsy, her sass, and her bravado rolled inside a fresh loaf of sourdough bread, slithering across roasted vegetables laced with slow drizzling balsamic, baked inside a piping hot strawberry rhubarb pie. The stories were alive inside the food. Imani loved food. Imani loved to feed people so her stories became the food itself . . . roasted with superfluous green garlic, cilantro, cumin, basil, a rack of lamb Imani threatened to throw at her brother one Easter, the duck medallions I cooked for the last Christmas meal of her life with us, or the wild salmon steaks she'd hide in the freezer.

What I know that I know is food heals. Food covers the wounded heart. Food holds the raging storm and invites Spirit to the table:

> I will love you anyway
> Even if you cannot stay,
> I think you are the one for me,
> Here is where you ought to be,
> I just want to satisfy you

Though you're not mine,
I can't deny you.
Don't you hear me talking baby?
Love me now or I'll go crazy.
—*Chaka Khan*

Appearance. Taste. Texture. Symbolism. Succulence. The Inter-action of Colors. The Dance. Behind Oven Doors. Edible Meta-phors. Velvety. Heavy Cream. Spice Jars. Simmer. Pan Fry. Cold Wash. Knead. Roll. Curl. Caramelize. Braise. Soak. Stir. Roast. Open Fire. Hot Oil. Blend. Fold. Mortar and Pestle. Pine Nuts. Raspber-ries. Almonds. Champagne Grapes. Mango Preserves. Muscadines. Tomatoes. Espresso. Le Coq au Vin. Charred Romaine. Mousse. Rose Water. Artichokes. Truffles. Butter. Candied Ginger. Chocolate. Dirty Rice. Brie. Cherries. Figs. Saffron Threads. Cinnamon. Nutmeg. Chutney. Parfait. Hazelnuts. Orange Peel. Lime Zest. Garlicky Col-lards. Ambrosia. Chow Chow. Red Rice. Rosemary Sea Salt.

I love the way these words, sounds, and ancient cooking rhythms sing inside my mouth . . . and honey chile don't forget the Honey.

If you really want to make a friend, go to someone's house and eat with him. The people who give you their food give you their heart. —*Cesar Chavez*

I remember the first meal I ever prepared for my husband. Lots of talking and long glances over a table full of lush sensuality. Mango gazpacho. Grilled salmon with a black bean, ginger-garlic glaze. Roasted asparagus. Brussel sprouts, beets, feta, and walnuts drizzled with fig balsamic vinaigrette. Basmati rice. Yeast rolls. Arugula salad. Spar-kling pear cider. Mixed berries dusted with coriander.

Once upon a time, I prepared a "last supper" for a lover I was kicking to the curb. It seemed best to leave a taste of me on his lips. Fillet of beef in puff pastry and Madeira cream sauce. Caramelized shallots, carrots, and mushrooms. Roasted lemon garlic artichokes. Grand Marnier cheesecake.

My first memory of a romantic meal was sharing a tomato sandwich made from tomatoes I'd grown in a small bucket as a child with a little boy visiting my grandmother. I was mesmerized by his seersucker-plaid shorts and matching bow tie. Crisp white shirt. White crew socks. White bucks. Magic happened between us when the juicy tomato dripped down his long elegant hands and he slowly licked the essence of my first harvest.

My husband and I love to cook. Our food landscape is forever changing, moving, reinventing itself, but what remains always is *sauce* so rich and soulful that it requires the licking of fingers, eyelids, noses, jellyroll laughs, and oceans of soft fluttery kisses. Our food adventures continue to awaken our passion . . .

Your stature is like that of the palm, and your breasts like clusters of fruit. I said, "I will climb the palm tree; I will take hold of its fruit." May your breasts be like the clusters of the vine, the fragrances of your breath like apples, and your mouth like the best wine. May the wine go straight to my lover, flowing gently over lips and teeth. I belong to my lover, and his desire is for me.
—*Song of Songs 7:7–10*

We stroll into each other's perfumed gardens gathering wild honeycomb. Whether dining by candlelight in our intimate dining room or sitting at a makeshift table in the woods with dandelions my love has picked on the way, we savor the bread between us. The anticipation of a romantic meal is oftentimes aphrodisiac enough. We can't stop smiling and casting knowing glances at each other the whole time we are preparing the meal. Late at night I flow through celestial whipped dreamy clouds trailing the scents of rose and lavender as I fold gently into the crevices of pillows stuffed with crushed rosemary.[1]

1. According to ancient scribes, rosemary was a love potion for engaged or married couples, symbolizing remembrance and fidelity.

JAKI SHELTON GREEN, the first North Carolina Piedmont Laureate, has published numerous collections of poetry, including *Dead on Arrival, Conjure Blues, Masks, singing a tree into dance, breath of the song,* and *feeding the light.* Her work has appeared in such publications as *Ms., Essence,* and *The Crucible.* She is the recipient of the North Carolina Award for Literature, the Kathryn H. Wallace Award for Artists in Community Service, and the Sam Ragan Award. She is an inductee into the N.C. Literary Hall of Fame.

Remembering the Cake

✸ JILL McCORKLE ✸

IN MY EARLIEST memory, I am sitting in my grandmother's deep kitchen sink with late afternoon light filling her small kitchen. The water is warm and soapy and I keep finding the slippery bar and raising it to my mouth only to have my grandmother take it away and place it back in the soap dish on the lip of the sink. It is a game we repeat many times, her head shaking as she says, *no no no.*

There is a window over the sink and it looks out on the driveway, a rising incline from Chippewa Street up to my grandmother's back porch. I would look out that window many times over the years while waiting for one of my parents to come and pick me up, or while seated on the counter watching my grandmother cook. She and I once rode in a taxi to a place called Kash & Karry to buy a hog head, and this is where I sat and watched her dismantle it and then do all kinds of things with the various parts I knew then (and now) I wanted nothing to do with. Her brother, Walter, loved the brain and my dad, much to my horror, liked hog head cheese. I watched her take the little paring knife she was partial to and scoop out the eyeballs, an act I found so horrifying I remember squealing with nervous laughter, wanting to look away but not being able.

There were always African violets on the windowsill. There was always something good in the oven, on the stove, in the refrigerator: fried apple pies, and chicken and pastry, oyster stew, fried chicken, pimento cheese, pound cake, whipped cream. My sister, cousins, and I argued over who got to lick the bowl and the beaters when one of her desserts was in the making.

My grandmother was always dressed in corset and stockings and a cotton "frock," and this is how she looked whether working in the garden where she grew enough vegetables to can and freeze and feed us all through the winter, or walking across the street to Hinds Grocery—an old brick building that still stands, at that time with a sawdust-covered floor and big jars of johnnycakes and penny candies and more of those things I swore to *never eat*: pickled things—eggs, pig feet. She looked the same from sunrise to sunset—sometimes her dress sprinkled with the black dirt of her garden and other times flour from the kitchen. There was always a fresh, very similar dress waiting for the next day. Her manner was like her body—soft and easy and calm, voice rarely rising. The only time I heard her upset was when one of her beloved African violets came crashing from the windowsill (I do recall that I was somehow involved in this happening) and she said *Jesus, God, Jesus,* a cry that seemed to silence the whole world until all was swept up and back in order and the calm, soothing voice returned.

But in the memory, other than the whisper of her sweet *no no no,* all I recall is the red and white polka-dot bowl on the counter. I am fixed on that bowl, the bright red dots, and on the warmth of the water and the slippery bar of soap. That bowl is what I most wanted when we all picked among her things after she died. I learned then that it had been a wedding present to my parents in 1951 and had somehow wound up in my grandmother's kitchen and never left, a permanent place there under the beaters of her freestanding mixer in the corner of her counter by the sink. I rarely used the bowl, always very careful with it, until one day when putting it away it slipped from my hands and onto the kitchen floor and into several pieces. My daughter was three at the time and this is one of *her* earliest memories, the first time she ever saw me cry. I put my head on the floor and sobbed until it occurred to me that though I was in that moment a child brought to a new place of mourning the loss of someone so dear and important in my life in so many ways, I was also a mother with a daughter standing spellbound and unsure what to do, a small hand on my back.

I told her it was okay. It was just a bowl. What I was really crying about was missing my grandmother. I saved the pieces—still have them—but then soon there was eBay, which featured hard-to-find Fire-King red and white polka-dot bowls. Now I have the broken pieces as well as a whole collection.

It was around this same time I began trying to duplicate my grandmother's pound cake, remembering vividly the batter she let us lick from the bowl, the way she lined the pan with a perfect circle of wax paper, the way she sifted and folded in blueberries in late summer. This cake is not for the faint-of-fat. Swans Down cake flour and eggs and sugar and butter and vanilla. The secret ingredient is Crisco.

Now the cake is second nature to me, the steps of the process near autopilot. I visit my mom often in a nursing facility two hours away in my hometown and almost every time I take a pound cake. Now it is something many of the staff members look forward to, and I give the recipe away often. But my real reason for bringing the cake is that my mother loves it, and I remind her each time that it is her mother's recipe—a cake served on birthdays, iced and decorated for those occasions, and now too many years and candles to ever count; it was taken to the beach on vacation, bake sales for school, always on the dessert table for every family holiday, and often just there on my grandmother's kitchen counter under the cake tin cover, something else in my possession.

Sometimes when I visit my mom, she knows who I am; other times, I am a friend of hers from high school or a cousin long dead, and more and more frequently, I am her mother. At a time when memories come and go, often with little rhyme or reason, she seems to always remember the cake, and by way of that, she remembers her mother and sometimes even her childhood home.

"Mama? Did you make this cake?" she asks.

"Yes I did," I tell her. "I've been making this cake for years."

The Annie Collins Pound Cake

Preheat oven to 350°. Grease pound cake pan (I usually cut a piece of wax paper to line bottom which is especially important if you ever do the blueberry version).

3   cups Swans Down cake flour (if you can't find, a cookbook
        can give you conversion info)
3   cups sugar
1   stick butter, softened
1   cup Crisco (YES! The secret ingredient—I buy the sticks.)
1   cup milk
5   eggs
½   teaspoon salt
½   teaspoon baking powder
1   teaspoon vanilla extract

Put in mixer and mix—fold into cake pan. If you want to add blueberries, take ¾ to 1 cup of berries (pat dry after washing) and fold around top, lightly pressing into batter. I have also done it with raspberries.

Bake anywhere from an hour to an hour and fifteen minutes, depending on your oven. Fork-test it; the top should be brown with that wonderful crust it makes! You want it done but not overly dry—might take a little experimenting with your oven. Also, if you add berries, it will take longer and is a little harder to judge.

Otherwise, it is foolproof!

I would add, do not forget to lick bowl and mixer as well as scrape what will be on the centerpiece of pan after removing—best part!

JILL McCORKLE is the author of ten books, including *Life After Life, Going Away Shoes, The Cheerleader,* and *July 7th.* Six of her books have been selected as New York Times Notable Books. She is the recipient of the North Carolina Award for Literature, the John Dos Passos Prize for Excellence in Literature, and many other awards. She teaches at the Bennington College MFA in Writing program.

Ruby's Kitchen

* WAYNE CALDWELL *

MY MOTHER RUBY'S life was dogged with sorrow and disappointment. She lost two brothers, one to influenza (he was twenty) and another to alcohol (that took a while—he outlived not only Ruby but also his twin children, both of whom drank themselves to death). Her father died of liver troubles the year after she married Troy Caldwell. Their marriage was childless for sixteen years—they adopted me after WWII. Troy joined the army early in 1942, leaving Ruby to care for her ailing mother and his aging parents. Her mother and Troy's father died in 1944–45, leaving her to look after a cranky mother-in-law. Shortly after Troy's return, a lump in his neck announced Hodgkin's disease. Although he lived nineteen more years, his last two or three were full of suffering. Six months after Troy died, I fled to Chapel Hill and left Ruby alone.

Perhaps a recipe to make a bitter old woman.

She *was* something of a pessimist, but I'd rather call her outlook an Appalachian fatalism that knows life is hard, you work until you die, and every silver lining has a cloud. Then God, who after all is in charge, rewards and punishes. But she was not bitter—far from it. I have an idea her new kitchen saved her from that.

My parents had lived in rentals since they married in 1932. The only one I know much about was in Candler Heights. Formerly the Hominy Baptist parsonage, it was a two-story clapboard house with an afterthought kitchen—high-ceilinged, dark, drafty, and dusty from wood range and laundry heater. Single light bulb dangled from the ceiling. This was where they brought me home in 1948, when I was six weeks old.

I bet when Troy came home from the Pacific, Ruby looked at him and said, "I want my own place. Get busy."

So he and her brother (yes, the alcoholic, who in those days stayed sober for months at a time and was a decent carpenter, welder, and electrician) built a house in the Sand Hill section. We moved into it in May 1949, a couple of weeks before my first birthday.

※ ※ ※

THE MOVE FROM Candler to Sand Hill meant changing churches. Ruby was raised a Baptist—her parents and brother were buried in the Hominy Church cemetery. Although Troy was born a Methodist, he had made do with Hominy's ways. But because Oak Forest Presbyterian was a gentle Sunday walk from their new home, they joined the Calvinists.

I expect Ruby found relief there. Baptist covenants are quite specific about such sins as drinking and dancing, demanding that Christians deny fellowship to topers and hoofers. Presbyterian covenants tend to leave such decisions to the Presbytery, Synod, or, in extreme cases, God. Ruby held that all sinners stand in need of prayer. And pound cake. Don't kick them out, feed them.

※ ※ ※

THE NEW HOUSE faced the rising sun, but the important view was west, both for sunsets and the prospect of Troy's garden, nearly half an acre. It fed Ruby's kitchen from March until October, rhubarb to pumpkins, radishes to turnips. We also relished Ruby's flower garden, a plot full of columbines, larkspurs, snapdragons, sweet Williams, hydrangeas, roses, asters, mums, you name it. Troy grew food, Ruby grew flowers. Ruby cooked, Troy ate. Every now and then he washed dishes. Seemed like a fine arrangement.

The house itself was four rooms. The north two were about fif-

teen by fifteen, the south pair slightly smaller because a skinny bathroom fought for a few square feet between them. The kitchen filled
the northwest quadrant and had three windows, one over a north-
facing sink. Peeling potatoes there, you could see who pulled up in
the driveway or what the neighbors were up to. A back door and two
west windows meant mellow afternoon light. The back door? Well,
only salesmen, census takers, or Jehovah's Witnesses called at our
front door. Family and friends entered our house via Ruby's efficient
kitchen.

Jutting out halfway down its west wall was her food bar, a counter-
height cabinet some foot and a half wide, drawers and doors on
the right. In the cabinet she kept mixer, meat grinder, cherry pitter,
pressure cooker, toaster, waffle iron. In the drawers lived household
stuff—pliers, tack hammer, screwdrivers, electrical tape, fuses, batteries, matches, ballasts (the ceiling fixture powered a pair of two-foot
fluorescent tubes), mousetraps. Its rounded front sported two shelves,
one holding a snow globe and the other a vase with dried flowers.

Atop the bar a radio, always tuned to WWNC, huddled against
the back wall. Mornings we heard Reid Wilson read obituaries, talk
about the weather, and tell of school closings. *The Romance of Helen
Trent* aired at twelve thirty and *Our Gal Sunday* at twelve forty-five,
during which a little boy showed out at his peril. A green Depression
glass bowl held what fruit was in season. Plus bananas. A cake saver
usually sat beside the fruit bowl.

Two steps took her from food bar to counter and cabinets to the
left of the sink. Underneath the first west window was a marble slab
for making mint candies. The upper cabinets held sugar, flour, baking
soda, cornmeal, salt, cornstarch, Crisco, food coloring, spices, bowls,
measuring cups, coffee, chocolate chips. Drawers contained measuring spoons, candy thermometer, tongs, meat forks, ice cream scoops.
Easy as pie to whip up a coconut cake there.

Cabinets to the right of the sink held dishes and flatware, dish-
towels and washrags, napkins and, in the very back of the top shelf, a
pint of Seagram's Seven. For colds. (Odd memory: Atop that cabinet

sat a shallow wooden bowl in which lay a straight razor—probably my father's, maybe his father's before that.) Her ceramic cookie jar, about the size of a soccer ball, almost always was full. Beside it, a loaf of sliced white bread.

The east wall held a four-eye electric range, a thin metal cabinet—for store-bought canned goods, TV Time popcorn, raisins, prunes, Kool-Aid, Jell-O, Karo Syrup—and a well-stocked refrigerator, atop which lived a flyswatter. Then a door to the living room.

To the left of the food bar was our dinette—gray Formica top, chrome-plated legs, one leaf. Best I remember we had four matching vinyl upholstered chairs, maybe six. (Not much room in this nook.) At this table we ate, pasted S&H Green Stamps into premium booklets, and studied our Sunday school lessons.

Beside the table a door led to the basement, which, in so small a house, became my favorite room. As a kid I used to roll around its concrete floor inside a metal barrel, which I'm sure drove Ruby nuts. When we replaced the living room sofa with a hide-a-bed and moved the old piece to the basement, I had a quiet, private place to read.

From Ruby's point of view, the basement was for washday. *Indoors!* A wringer washer and clothesline made rainy Mondays bearable. She also had bushels of winter storage room for sweet potatoes and onions, plus shelves for home-canned goods—pickles of every description, to-matoes, tomato juice, string beans, and jams and jellies. This, along with a huge freezer in the garage—full of beef, fish, vegetables, and fruit—meant we might survive years of famine, war, and pestilence, none of which Ruby would have been much surprised to see.

On the north wall sat her mother's ancient wood range she used infrequently for summer canning. I think she kept it to remind her of the good old days she had, thankfully, left behind.

I can only imagine how tickled she was to fix and serve the first meal in her new kitchen. And the first pound cake? Golly, she must have thought she'd died and gone to heaven.

※　※　※

I LIKED "HELPING" in the kitchen when I was little. At first, drumming on pots with wooden spoons. Then stirring stuff, counting out a dozen maraschinos for cherry wink cookies, cutting mints when I was old enough to handle scissors. I loved to lick spoons clean—cake batter, deviled eggs, chocolate icing. To remember the taste of her raw biscuit dough still brings a tear. In Ruby's kitchen, warm in winter, hot in summer, I felt safe and loved. And full. Which, to her, were much the same.

*   *   *

TWO OF RUBY'S cookbooks have survived. A standard-issue *Good Housekeeping* loose-leaf notebook covered in a red and white gingham pattern, heavily used. And a Blue Horse composition book bought in the late Fifties for forty-nine cents. In it she pasted recipes for all manner of sweets, as well as pickles, sauces, punches, breads, and salads, clipped from newspaper, *Parade*, *Southern Living*, *Farm Journal*. A couple are mimeographed. But most are in blue or green ink in Ruby's neat hand. With comments: "try at Christmas"; "what to do with leftover mashed potatoes."

It's a wonder I have a tooth in my head—to think how many tons of sugar passed through Ruby's kitchen almost puts me into a diabetic coma. I wouldn't be surprised if the sheriff suspected her of making liquor in the basement.

Interesting as these recipes are, they are more revealing for their sources, proof that Ruby's kitchen by the Sixties had become a neighborhood hub.

We have Mollie Gorman's chili sauce from way down Oakview Road; Madeline Gudger's butter mints from Scratch Ankle; Elizabeth Siler's green tomato pickles from Sand Hill School Road; Lillian Dillingham's fruit cake cookies from Enka Village; Mrs. Clayman's brownies (the pastor's wife was Ida Mae but I never heard her referred to as anything but Mrs. Clayman) from a mile down Sand Hill Road; Sadie Brookshire's Ranger cookies from Grandview; Edna Roberts's limewater pickles, again down Sand Hill. Ruby's immediate range was a square mile or more. Add family and old friends, this became a county. Big territory for a woman who never learned to drive.

Ruby's notebook is a treasury of cooking wisdom gleaned from many sources. Old church, old friends, new church, new friends, sharing the good news that here is food—take, eat, it's good for you. Even—or maybe especially—German chocolate cake.

I won't say Ruby's kitchen was her church or her cookbook her Bible. She wasn't much for metaphor, and would have thought to confuse a cookbook with the Bible bad taste, if not outright blasphemy. But her kitchen certainly was her sanctuary. From it she spread love—and food—all over the neighborhood. How often did a neighbor or relative drop in for a chat—have coffee and lemon meringue pie—and return rested and stronger? Minister, counselor, therapist, baker, cook, all folded into Ruby Caldwell.

She considered herself one of the least, but I am confident that when Jesus gets around to sorting sheep from goats, Ruby will be on his right. We were hungry and thirsty, after all, and she gave us food and drink. Advice and hospitality. Good, nourishing fare from Ruby's kitchen.

WAYNE CALDWELL is the author of two novels, *Cataloochee* and *Requiem by Fire*, winner of the 2010 Thomas Wolfe Memorial Literary Award from the WNC Historical Association. In 2013, the Fellowship of Southern Writers honored him with their James Still Award for excellence in writing about the Appalachian South. He has also written a number of short stories, one of which appeared in Eno Publishers' *27 Views of Asheville*, and poems.

So, a Yankee Walks into a North Carolina Kitchen . . .

☀ FRAN McCULLOUGH ☀

I DO ACTUALLY have some Southern credentials. Born in Quantico, Virginia, where my one hundred percent Irish father was a colonel stationed with the Marine Corps, I was four when he was transferred from a brief stint in San Diego to Parris Island, South Carolina. There, I spent two happy years inhaling the mysterious fragrance of the Spanish moss hung on live oaks along the shell-lined dirt roads. I learned Stephen Foster songs and wept as I sang "Old Black Joe" for the sad fate of the slaves whose descendants were everywhere I looked—so different from San Diego. And of course the food was completely different from what we'd eaten out West; we were in grits country now. It was a real place, even a dangerous one, where a girl about my age had recently fallen into the quicksand that surrounded the island. She suffocated and died, as my father reminded me every time we drove past the spot.

Every military brat knows that you dive into the life around you wherever you are, because in a year or two years or three (if you're lucky), you'll be packed off someplace else, and then you're headlong into the new life. The next life for us was in the suburbs of Washington, DC, and we weren't eating things like spoon bread and fried cornmeal mush and fresh biscuits anymore. I remember prim apple butter sandwiches with peanut butter and gray Salisbury steaks. At school when I was called on to read out loud from a Dick and Jane reader, my heavy South Carolina accent was gleefully mocked with howls of laughter—and I murdered it, understanding right away that it signaled I was stupid.

Somewhere in my alligator brain, though, that accent lives on, along with the memories of the soul-filling food we ate in the Carolina Lowcountry. The minute I start an involving conversation with a native Southerner, that accent returns, light at first and then a bit more insistent. Inevitably Southerners start talking about food, and then we're off and running.

I spent a couple of decades living all over the world—from a tiny island in the South Pacific to Hawaii to Northern California, where I mainly grew up—before I set out for New York to work in book publishing. But here I am back in the South, near Chapel Hill, North Carolina. It's a place that can seem more like New Hampshire than South Carolina, a bit reserved compared to the more raucous state to the south. Novelist Elizabeth Spencer suggests it may be the calming influence of the area's original Quaker and Presbyterian settlers. I arrived about ten years ago, quite sure I knew a lot about Southern food because I'd edited some important Southern cookbooks, had attended Southern food conferences, and had a wide circle of friends in the food world elite who'd educated me on the fly. When I got to Hillsborough and environs, however, I didn't find exactly what I expected.

For one thing, I had no idea Southern food is so micro-regional. What I knew about one foodway wasn't at all true here or in various other places. The fish—triggerfish, black drum, spots—are entirely different from the Yankee fish or Southern fish elsewhere; fresh dill is often missing altogether in the markets; what people really focus on is vegetables—quite the opposite from their cartoon profile of being profligate gobblers of fat and sugar.

No one had told me about the giant heads of collard greens that seem to belong in a stroller rather than a market bag, or the flat bunches of collard leaves that look like the fans they hand out at funerals. People here tend to crave unpromising vegetables like cabbage and yellow crookneck squash. It never seems to occur to them to use the highly nutritious sweet potato greens (despite George Washington Carver's entreaties that they do so), free for the taking and on the menu elsewhere in the world,. And why are some green tomatoes so deliciously acidy when you fry them and others in the same batch have all the flavor of Styrofoam?

Then there are the little-known seasonal sensations. I heard somewhere about Ridgeway melons, really just regular old cantaloupes that grow in a magical sandy clay soil that's only about eight miles square, up on the Virginia border near Warrenton. Early July to early August is their brief time, and in the old days they used to be loaded onto trains for their big trip north to the Waldorf Astoria. They're unbelievably delicious, and if I can't manage to get up to the roadside stands for them, I can often find them at the vintage King's Red & White grocery in Durham—and nowhere else.

It was the first week in August that my chef friend Aaron Vandemark brought me a fat ripe wild pawpaw, found growing near the Eno River not too far away. I thought pawpaws might be mythological or extinct, but this magnificent specimen was all too real, intensely and unidentifiably tropical as three of us savored it icy cold, its unctuous flesh scooped up with silver spoons.

August had another surprise for me. I was thrilled to find little fresh butter beans at the local farmers market. I bought some from the Walker Farm's stand at the market and cooked them as I would lima beans in New York. I know this is one of those iconic Southern dishes, and yet mine were about as exciting as a frozen dinner. After several more disappointing efforts, I decided to ask Gaye Walker at the market how she does it.

Well, she said, it's pretty simple. You have to start with a little meat, like bacon or ham or a ham hock, and you want a little onion in there, and then you add your butter beans and some salt and pepper and water to cover and just cook them slowly for a long time. What's a long time? Well, she cooks hers for three *hours* for the flavor to really get into the beans, though they're cooked through after an hour and a half. But her daughter says they're ready to eat after two hours. I was stunned. And skeptical.

I bought more butter beans and tried again, checking after an hour and a half. They were fantastic. I summoned my husband, who loathes lima beans, and he agreed they were delicious. I let them go the whole three hours and I couldn't say if they were better cooked longer or not. So I started asking my Southern food gurus for their opinions on how to cook better butter beans.

Something I especially love about Southern cooking is the intensity of the hothead fights people have over food and how it should be prepared. Ask several Southern cooks in the same room how they make pimento cheese and there will be mayhem. Expatriate North Carolinian James Villas, who always loves a good argument, has written several cookbooks with his mother, Martha Pearl, in which they battle in print over the right way to cook this or that. In anticipation of getting butter beans right sooner or later, I had bought and frozen about six pounds of them for future experiments. *No no no!* said Jean Anderson, Chapel Hill author of *A Love Affair with Southern Cooking,* a treasury of authentic recipes. You have to *blanch* the butter beans first for a few minutes before you freeze them because they contain an enzyme that can spoil the dish of beans. Oh. Jean studied food science at Cornell, and she knows her beans. I checked further with John Martin Taylor, author of *Hoppin' John's Lowcountry Cooking,* and he concurred—and added that his butter beans have only cured meat and beans in them. I'd have to wait another year to work out the recipe and toss the butter beans cooling their heels in my freezer. When I told Jim Villas this sad news, he strongly disagreed and insisted I should go right ahead and cook the beans, never mind any cautionary tales about enzymes. I'm here to tell you Villas is right: You can just toss the plastic freezer bag of shelled butter beans you buy at the farmers market directly into the freezer for a midwinter treat.

Butter beans belong to the huge family of beans and peas, and there are hundreds upon hundreds of varieties. In late July and August farmers markets offer cream peas, lady peas, Dixie peas, and butter beans of all stripes, including speckled (also known as calicos)— pretty, but not considered to be high on the flavor flagpole, though not as scorned as black-eyed peas often are. People pass along seeds of black butter beans or purple ones. Fresh tiny green flat butter beans, the ones I look for, are called Sieva beans—pronounced *sivvy* beans in South Carolina—while their large white or cream-colored cousins that are dried at harvest are almost always called butter beans, confusingly. When you find the little ones fresh, grab them and tuck them away in the freezer, ready to be turned into one of the South's most glorious dishes. Or double the recipe and freeze them freshly cooked, then defrost up to several months later in the fridge before reheating to serve, as John Martin Taylor does.

You can grow your own Sieva beans from the same rootstock Thomas Jefferson had at Monticello. The shop at Monticello sometimes has them. Or go to Southern Exposure Seed Exchange website, click on pole beans, and you'll find Sieva (Carolina) pole lima beans. Southern Exposure also stocks the seeds for greasy beans, which I've never even seen, never mind tasted, but they have a devoted following.

Here's my current favorite way with butter beans. You can leave out the garlic, the cayenne, and the sugar for a purist version. I've substituted smoked Spanish paprika (pimenton) for the cayenne with great results, and lots of people prefer their butter beans with Texas Pete hot sauce—which is from North Carolina, not Texas, despite its sassy name and the cowboy on the label. You can also use supermarket frozen baby lima beans if you have no other alternative.

Better Butter Beans

SERVES 4 TO 6

3 slices of bacon, roughly cut in small pieces
½ onion, diced
1 garlic clove, minced or pressed
1 pound little fresh-shelled green butter beans or defrosted
   frozen
   salt and pepper to taste
⅛ teaspoon cayenne
½ teaspoon sugar
   a little more bacon grease, if needed

Put the bacon pieces in a large pot and fry to release the bacon grease. Remove the cooked bacon and reserve. Cook the diced onion gently with the garlic in the bacon grease over medium heat until the onion is transparent.

Add the butter beans and about 1½ quarts of water or enough to cover the beans by an inch or two. Bring to a boil, then reduce the heat to low and cook slowly uncovered until the beans are tender (about an hour). Don't let it boil. Check every 20 minutes or so to see if you need to add more water. Stir in the bacon pieces, cayenne, and sugar. Taste for salt and pepper, sugar and heat, and stir gently.

Taste the beans again. See if they need a little something, like more bacon grease. Once they taste right, you can keep them warm in a slow cooker on the lowest setting, covered. They'll just get more delicious the longer they cook, even several hours, but check every now and then to be sure there's enough water.

That's it. Except for one thing: There's a deep, bring-you-to-your-knees taste that memorable Southern food has, especially vegetables. It's partly seasoning, partly endlessly tasting and correcting,

and partly something ineffable. I first experienced the importance
of that last factor when I went to an out-of-the-way black restaurant
in Charleston that I'd heard had great collards, a new vegetable for
me at the time. The collards were indeed transporting, and I asked
the waitress if I could get the recipe. "You can," she said, "but I got
to tell you, I got the recipe from our cook and I made them and they
didn't taste like hers. So I asked her again and she said the recipe was
right and she showed me. But you know, she has an old hand, and I
don't." Me neither.

I found another old hand in Savannah when I was the writer for a
cookbook by Dora Charles, the black cook who worked for so many
years in Paula Deen's restaurant kitchen. Dora has taught nearly a
hundred people to cook but had never written down her own family
recipes, passed along to her by her grandmother when Dora was six.
Dora is meticulous in her kitchen prep and in her seasoning. And
one way or another, there's usually a little bacon grease in whatever
she's cooking.

You would think that everything would end up tasting sort of the
same, but it doesn't; somehow the bacon brings out the inherent flavor of the ingredients themselves. Dora always has a little pot of
bacon grease by her stovetop and uses it the way a French chef adds
a spoonful of cream: to carry the flavors and bring them together. It's
a great finishing touch for butter beans.

One thing the old hands like Dora know is that you need to work
a dish so it has the right taste: For butter beans, I like it a little smoky,
a little spicy, a little creamy from the beans themselves, but with the
beans still holding together perfectly. If you let them boil once they've
started cooking, they'll get mealy and start to fall apart. I swear a
wooden spoon will help to keep them whole, but stir them very gently, only as much as you need to as they slowly slowly inch their way
toward glory.

FRAN McCULLOUGH is a longtime editor of literary books and cookbooks in New York, mainly at Harper's and The Dial Press. She is the first recipient of the Roger Klein Award for Creative Editing. She is the author of *Good Fat,* an investigation into the healthfulness of the fats we eat, as well as *The Low-Carb Diet Cookbook.* She edited the "Best American Recipes" series of annual cookbooks from 1999 to 2007. She received a James Beard Award for her recipe anthology, *Great Food Without Fuss,* co-edited with Barbara Witt. She now lives and cooks in Hillsborough.

An Onslow County Tradition

☀ LENARD D. MOORE ☀

WHEN I WAS growing up, eating good food was a family tradition, especially the delicious choices for all at any gathering. Mostly there were vegetables steaming and waiting for us, but there were some raw ones too, freshly picked, sliced, and neatly arranged on plates— onions, cucumbers, and tomatoes. All of them were from our backyard garden, each appealing to the taste of my parents, siblings, and me.

This celebration of food, of course, began with the seeds that my father and I purchased from the farm supplies store. I also received seeds from my great-grandmother and great-aunt who knew I gardened each year and that I knew how to take care of a garden because I learned from them, as well as my father. I remember the joy of turning the soil with a shovel, making furrows with the garden hoe, planting, hilling, and watering the seeds or plants that needed hand-setting, such as collards, cabbage, and tomato slips. I learned how to transplant corn from my great-grandmother, including what to do with the long leaves.

I tended the garden—weeding, watering, and raking—until the waist-high and shoulder-high plants yielded their output. Always on the ground cucumber, watermelon, and cantaloupe vines sprawled all over the plot. Pole beans wrapped around the slender poles. Of course, I worried about deer and rabbits nibbling whatever they wanted in the garden, but I also learned how to build a scarecrow from my great-grandmother and great-aunt. I recall how scarecrows guarded my great-grandmother's corn and peanut fields while my brothers and I chopped grass away from the long rows in the stifling sun. We worked, talked, joked, and laughed, but we paid attention to our chopping, keeping our eyes focused.

Like others in our African American community, we often ate from our garden. There was no talk of going to the grocery store for vegetables. After harvesting what we wanted from the garden, we sat on the front porch where we snapped or shelled beans and shucked corn with our father. All we knew was eating fresh food out of the garden.

In my early years, another one of our great-aunts taught my brothers and me how to fish—the baiting, casting, and reeling in the catch—for one big enough to take off the hook and place in the bucket. She would pick us up and drive us to the fishing spots, mostly the Atlantic Ocean where the breaking blue-gray water seemed to whisper to us. It was beautiful. It was calming. It was happiness.

In those same years, my great-grandmother, my grandmother, and my uncle raised chickens. Another one of my uncles raised pigs. Thus there was fresh meat, too. So the community was packed with food, despite the eye-burning sweat from all of the work that it took to put food on our table.

Later years far into adulthood, my youngest sister would ask, "Do you remember when Dad Dad would have sweat dripping off him while cooking for us?"

"Yes," I said, picturing the cooking scene vividly. That's how it was. It seemed like he enjoyed cooking in that hot kitchen. In fact, I knew that he knew what fatherhood was all about, and he demonstrated how to be a good provider and a great father. At breakfast, his favorite dish often steamed in front of us. I can still smell those fried potatoes and onions. They were delicious.

Perhaps, I should have said that I learned how to clean fish from my grandfather. I scaled, gutted, and cleaned the flounder, trout, spot, or croaker. I can still picture the silver pan piled with fish in it, smelling of the sea, on the long, wooden table in the backyard. Then, in early evening, our mother fried the fish and made hot-water cornbread. At any moment, we might push through the black swinging doors into the kitchen so that we could smell the aroma of supper.

Supper, which is what we called the evening meal, consisted of fresh cooked collards, baked macaroni and cheese, hot fish, and cornbread. There was freshly picked hot pepper, which was diced for the collards, and hot sauce for the fish. Sometimes our mother baked a pineapple upside-down cake. We were well fed. So it was typical to leave the table happy and content.

I am reeling with food memories. My sisters recently told some people how, in my late teens, I cooked for them, our whole family in fact. Yes, I learned to cook from our parents. I experimented with cooking different meals, too. I even had a recipe, "A la Beef Delight," published in a cookbook. I remember how my late daughter loved a particular dish that I cooked, which was barbecue chicken with steamed rice baked in it. I always made certain that there was enough sauce to drizzle over the rice. Like my father, I sliced fresh tomatoes, cucumbers, and onion, too. It was not difficult to keep the custom going, because my daughter enjoyed healthy meals. She also loved it when I grilled food in the backyard.

It still gives me pleasure to remember our eating together as a family. When my father arrived home from working at Camp Lejeune, we knew it was suppertime. Our mouths began to water. No one trickled to the table late.

Although my childhood home in Jacksonville was bulldozed earlier this decade to make room for the expansion of the highway, I still carry fond memories of family and food. It's bittersweet now, because my great-grandmother, grandmother, great-aunts, uncle, and my daughter have transitioned. Sadly, that roster of loss of kinfolk has grown. But food and the memory of food are still cherished in Eastern North Carolina.

LENARD D. MOORE is the author of *A Temple Looming* and *Forever Home,* among other books. He is the recipient of many awards, including the prestigious North Carolina Award, the Sam Ragan Fine Arts Award, the Indies Arts Award, and three-time recipient of the Haiku Museum of Tokyo Award. He is founder and executive director of the legendary Carolina African American Writers' Collective. A North Carolina native, he teaches African American literature and creative writing at the University of Mount Olive, where he is associate professor of English.

The Recipe Box

☀ LEE SMITH ☀

Excerpted from *Dimestore: A Writer's Life*

MY MOTHER'S RECIPE box sits on the windowsill in our North Carolina kitchen where my eye falls on it twenty, maybe thirty times a day. I will never move it. An anachronism in my own modern kitchen, the battered box contains my mother's whole life story, in a way, with all its places and phases, all her hopes and the accommodations she made in the name of love, as I have done, as we all do. I can read it like a novel—for in fact, our recipes tell us everything about us: where we live, what we value, how we spend our time. Mama's recipe box is an odd green-gold in color. She "antiqued" it, then decoupaged it with domestic decals of the Fifties: One depicts a rolling pin, a flour sifter, a vase of daisies, and a cheerful, curly-headed mom wearing a red bead necklace; another shows a skillet, a milk bottle, a syrup pitcher, three eggs, and a grinning dad in an apron.

Oh, who are these people? My father never touched a spatula in his life. My mother suffered from "bad nerves," also "nervous stomach." She lived mostly on milk toast herself, yet she never failed to produce a nutritious supper for my father and me, including all the food groups, for she had long been a home economics teacher. Our perfect supper was ready every night at six thirty, the time a family ought to eat, in Mama's opinion, though my workaholic daddy never got home from the dimestore until eight or nine at the earliest, despite his best intentions. Somewhere in that two-hour stretch, I would have been allowed to eat alone, reading a book—my favorite thing in the world. My mother would have had her milk toast. And when

my father finally had his solitary supper, warmed to an unrecogniz-
able crisp in the oven, he never failed to pronounce it "absolutely
delicious—the best thing I've ever put in my mouth!" My mother
never failed to believe him, to give him her beautiful, tremulous
smile, wearing the Fire and Ice lipstick she'd hurriedly applied when
she heard his car in the driveway. Well, they loved each other—two
sweet, fragile people who carefully bore this great love like a large
glass object, incredibly delicate, along life's path.

My mother's father had died when she was only three, leaving
a pile of debt and six children for my grandmother to raise alone
on Chincoteague Island. Grandma Annie Marshall turned their big
old Victorian home into a boardinghouse, and it was here in the
boardinghouse kitchen that my mother had learned to cook. Her
recipe box holds sixteen different recipes for oysters, including Oyster
Stew, Oyster Fritters, Oyster Pie, Scalloped Oysters, and the biblical-
sounding Balaam's Oysters. Clams are prepared "every whichaway,"
as she would have put it. There's also Planked Shad, Cooter Pie,
and Pine Bark Stew. Mr. Hop Biddle's Hush Puppies bear the nota-
tion, "tossed to the hounds around the campfire to keep them quiet."
Mama notes that the favorite breakfast at the boardinghouse was
fried fish, cornmeal cakes, and "plenty of hot coffee." These cornmeal cakes remained her specialty from the time she was a little girl,
barely able to reach the stove, until her death eighty-four years later
in the mountains so far from her island home. I imagine her as a
child, biting her bottom lip in concentration and wiping perspiration
off her pretty little face as she flips those cornmeal cakes on the hot
griddle. Later, I see her walking miles across the ice in winter, back
to college on the mainland.

Her lofty aspirations were reflected in her recipes: Lady Baltimore
Cake came from Cousin Nellie, who had "married well"; the hopeful Plantation Plum Pudding and Soiree Punch had both been contributed by my Aunt Gay-Gay in Birmingham, Alabama, the very
epitome of something Mama had desperately wanted to attain. She
wanted me to attain it, too, sending me down to Alabama every sum-

mer for Lady Lessons. The Asparagus Soufflé recipe came from my elegant Aunt Millie, who had married a Northern steel executive who actually cooked dinner for us himself, wearing an apron. He produced a roast beef that was bright red in the middle; at first I was embarrassed for him, but then it turned out he'd meant to do it that way all along; he thought red meat was good, apparently, and enjoyed wearing the apron.

Here are Mama's bridge club recipes, filed all together. My first idea of an elegant meal came from this bridge club, whose members met every Thursday at noon for lunch and bridge, rotating houses, for years and years until its members began to die or move to Florida. I can see Mama now, greeting her friends at the door in her favorite black-and-white polka-dot dress. I sat on the top stair to watch them arrive. I loved the cut flowers, the silver, and the pink cloths on the tables, though it was clear to me even then that the way these ladies were was a way I'd never be.

The food my mama gave the bridge club was wonderful. They feasted upon molded pink salad that melted on the tongue (back then I thought all salads were Jell-O salads); something called Chicken Crunch (cut-up chicken, mushroom soup, celery, water chestnuts, Chinese noodles); and Lime Angel Cloud. All the bridge lunch recipes required mushroom soup, Jell-O, Dream Whip, or pecans.

But the recipes Mama actually used most—these soft, weathered index cards covered with thumbprints and spatters—reflect her deep involvement with her husband's family and their Appalachian community: Venison Stew, Gaynor Owens' Soup Beans, Ava McClanahan's Apple Stack Cake, my grandmother's Methodist Church Supper Salad, and my favorite, Fid's Funeral Meat Loaf. A ham was also good in case of death, glazed with brown sugar and Coca-Cola. Mama's recipe for Salvation Cake had a Bible verse listed beside each ingredient (the almonds came from Genesis 43:11), and the only instruction given for baking was the cryptic Proverbs 23:14. Fat content was never a consideration. Biscuits called for lard, and Chocolate

Velvet Cake required one cup of mayonnaise. A hearty beef and cheese casserole was named Husband's Delight.

I, too, have written out my life in recipes. As a young bride, I had eleven dessert recipes featuring Cool Whip as the main ingredient. Then came the hibachi and fondue period, then the quiche and crepes phase, then pasta, and now it's these salsa years. Just this past Christmas, I made cranberry salsa for everybody. My mother would not have touched salsa—let alone sushi!—with a ten-foot pole. One time when we all went out for bagels in Chapel Hill, she said, "This may taste good to someone who has never eaten a biscuit." Another thing she used to say is, "No matter what is wrong with you, a sausage biscuit will make you feel a whole lot better." I agree, though I have somehow ended up with a wonderful husband who eats rare meat, wears an apron himself upon occasion, and makes a terrific risotto. We share the cooking. I seldom have time to bake these days, but I still make Mama's Famous Loaf Bread upon occasion, simply because the smell of it baking takes me straight back to that warm kitchen where somebody was always visiting. I can still hear my mother's voice, punctuated by her infectious laugh, her conspiratorial "Now promise me you won't tell a soul . . ."

On impulse I reach for Mama's recipe box and take out one of the most wrinkled and smudged, Pimento Cheese, everybody's favorite, thinking as always that I really ought to get these recipes into the computer, or at least copy them before they disintegrate completely. On this card, Mama underlined Durkee's Dressing, followed by a parenthesis: "(The secret ingredient!)" Though I would never consider leaving Durkee's Dressing out, I don't really believe it is the secret ingredient. The secret ingredient is love.

Mama's Famous Loaf Bread

2½ cups milk
3   tablespoons sugar
1   teaspoon salt
4   tablespoons Crisco

Scald the above ingredients together.

When lukewarm, add 2 well-beaten eggs and 2 packages dissolved yeast (in warm water). Add flour to make medium stiff dough. 7–8 cups—Let rise till double in bulk. Knead well. Shape into loaves in greased pans. Let rise—will double in size. Bake 350° about 35–40 minutes—until well browned. Grease loaves with margarine when you remove the pans. Cool completely.

Mama's Pimento Cheese

1   teaspoon mustard
1   4-ounce jar chopped pimentos, drained
¼   teaspoon cayenne pepper—just a pinch!
½   cup mayonnaise
¼   cup Durkee's Dressing
2   cloves garlic, minced (or a bit of onion if you don't like garlic)
1   pound cheddar cheese, grated

Mix together and refrigerate.

LEE SMITH is the author of thirteen novels, including *Guests on Earth* and *Fair and Tender Ladies,* and four short story collections, most recently, *Mrs. Darcy and the Blue-Eyed Stranger.* She has received numerous honors and awards, including an Academy Award in Fiction from the American Academy of Arts and Letters, the North Carolina Award for Literature, and the Sidney Lanier Prize for Southern Fiction. Her memoir *Dimestore* is her first book of nonfiction.

CAROLINA FLAVOR

Grape (Hull Pie) Expectations
on Highway 117

❋ CELIA RIVENBARK ❋

YOU COULD SMELL the barbecue long before you pulled into the parking lot at Norris's Restaurant in the little Duplin County town of Wallace.

Norris's barbecue was the greasiest, smokiest I ever ate and it was one of the main reasons I showed up on a fine May morning in 1974 to apply for a waitress job at the only sit-down restaurant in town. I needed money for community college in the fall and I knew there was no way I was going to work at Family Dollar store like my sister because just that week, right after she had promised to "put in a word" for me, she'd been given the unimaginable task of cleaning up a dressing room that an intoxicated shopper mistook for a bathroom. ("Walked right out of there and kept on shopping," she said later, still shaking her head at the memory.)

No thanks. In a way it was a good thing that my retail career was torpedoed. Because, truth be told, I wanted to work as close to my true love—fine, authentic Southern home-style cooking—as humanly possible. There was a "help wanted" sign in the window and Norris's was owned by a second cousin once removed so I figured I could always play the "cuz card" if need be. It wasn't fancy but there was an added-on paneled "Liberty Room" where the Rotary and Chamber of Commerce met, and it was also home to the town's only salad bar. Listen. I'm not talking about that freeze-dried, pre-bagged slop they put on a salad bar at McApple Tuesday's these days. This was the real deal: real homemade chicken, ham, tuna, and egg salads, framed by ice-cold containers of fresh beets, real devilled eggs, homemade pickles. I guess there was some lettuce.

"You Howard Lee's daughter?" asked Annie Faye Norris, the owner, who was fierce way before Beyonce. She was just as wide as she was tall and she didn't take any of that stuff they were still cleaning up over at the Family Dollar.

"Yes, ma'am," I said. "I wondered if I could get a job as a waitress. I've always loved y'alls'es food."

"Uh-huh." Clearly Annie Faye Norris didn't have time for flattery. My God, but her Grape Hull Pie was legendary. Even to this day, I purely swoon at the memory of those tender muscadine hulls, separated carefully from their pulp and seeds before being chopped fine, then reunited in a dense custard that was poured into a lard-built pastry as tender as a first kiss and topped with a good four inches of meringue.

Grape Hull Pie was a rare treat, awaited by the locals in Wallace like some more uppity folks might anticipate an exceptional Beaujolais Nouveau. It was only on the menu a couple of weeks out of the year. Labor intensive, weird, and wonderful. I've never seen it on a menu anywhere else and I'm almost glad because it could never be as good as Annie Faye's.

While I stood there and salivated at the thought of that pie, Annie Faye narrowed her eyes so that they were nearly lost in her round face. She looked me up and down for a full thirty seconds. Finally she sighed in what sounded like total resignation.

"Get yer hair out of your face and go get some newspapers and vinegar and start on those front windows."

Okay, you have to understand that I was used to Windex. I wasn't making the connection.

Dot, who was Annie Faye's chain-smoking sister and could elegantly stack six plates of bacon, eggs, and grits on her skinny forearms, took pity on me. "Best way to get a shiny window is newspaper and vinegar. Get to it."

So I did. And, bless Patty, they were right. After an hour or so, the plate-glass windows on the front of the little dining room were clean and streak-free. Sadly, my hands were completely black.

"No food service today," growled Dot on her way out to smoke her hundredth Kent of the morning. "Lookit yer hands."

It took an hour of scrubbing with Camay to get them clean again. Gloves. Yep. I was a brand-new graduate of Wallace-Rose Hill High School and didn't have sense enough to wear gloves when I was cleaning windows with newspapers and vinegar. At this point, I felt only marginally smarter than that poor confused soul in the Family Dollar dressing room.

The next morning, Day 2 of my first "public" job, I had bobby-pinned my hair out of my face and borrowed some thick white uniform pants and a matching top from my sister's short-lived career in something called respiratory therapy at the county hospital. ("I help them breathe," she had explained succinctly, while drawing on a Vantage menthol.)

"Your hair looks like a rat's nest," said Annie Faye, still cemented to her post at the cash register, just as I'd left her twelve hours before. Had she been there all night? She reminded me of those owls that people put on their houses to scare off woodpeckers. She never moved but she was working all the time.

Mercifully, a high school friend who had worked at the restaurant a couple of years was working the breakfast shift. Christy showed me how to roll my limp blonde hair over a tube sock and twist it into a passable bun. Amazing!

While I'd already learned a lot about previously unheard-of uses for newspapers and tube socks, I just wanted to work with the food. I wanted to holler "Order up!" to the cooks, Annie Faye's grown sons: William, who was only slightly warmer in demeanor than his mama, and Danny, the prankster whose determined cheer was enough to offset his mother's and brother's dour nature right by itself.

So far, restaurant work wasn't glamorous. I'd had enough talk about hair buns and window cleaning and wanted to, literally, see how the sausage was made. Most of all, I wanted to end the day sitting in the booth where the waitresses sat. They rolled silverware, counted their tips, and drank gallons of sweet tea. After work, you could help yourself to barbecued pork or chicken but no seafood. That stuff cost money, Annie Faye growled in a manner that I no longer took personally.

I was happy to mound up that barbecue on the plate. Because this was decades before there was a Food Network to tell me about the "bark" on barbecued pork, I didn't know what to call that fabulous crunchy, blackened substance that clung to the tenderloin. Yes, Norris's had bark in spades, and a town of 3,000 was all the happier for it. It didn't take long for me to realize that a lot of the regulars referred to "my second heart attack" or "lost my leg to the sugar," but no one felt the need to make any dietary adjustments.

With my hair bun finally approved, I was given a *guest check* pad and a pen to tuck inside my respiratory-therapy-turned-waitress pants. One of my first tables of the day left me two cents. They were buttholes.

Things got better, of course. I got pretty good at customer service, coyly twirling my pen in the air and reciting the specials. I knew the regulars and had their orders into William or Danny by the time they hit the door. Wallace had a surprisingly large Jewish population for a tiny town in Eastern North Carolina and Mr. Kramer was one of my favorite regulars. Every Friday, he came in with a newspaper to read and sat heavily into one of the avocado vinyl booths. Chicken livers and coffee. Nothing else. A sweet old lady who worked the *New York Times* crossword (and, therefore, was rumored to be a Communist) and drove the town's only Mercedes came in every afternoon for a fried egg sandwich on toast with mustard. One time, a Yankee came in by accident and started breastfeeding her toddler right there under the portrait of General Robert E. Lee. I'm not proud of it but I remember just standing there, my Bunn coffee pot mid-air, staring.

"What in the hell is she doing?" muttered Annie Faye. Never the most maternal type, she may not have actually known.

On Friday nights, especially during tobacco harvest season, the warehousemen would come in and order our most expensive meal: A porterhouse steak that was so big it hung off either end of the special black and silver platters we used so they would "sizzle." I loved saying, "Be careful, y'all; that platter's hot!" It made me feel like an insider. I could handle it but, well, maybe you couldn't.

Seafood was big, too, on Friday night. Norris's had a seafood platter that was called a *barge* and it had a ridiculous number of fried shrimp on it. Over the summer, I'd made friends with most of the other waitresses and cooks and they kept my shameful secret from Annie Faye. See, that thirty-shrimp barge never made it out of the kitchen intact. I took a two- or three-shrimp tax for myself before I busted through those swinging doors. Couldn't help myself.

At the end of the summer, I had to quit Norris's to go to school and I was sad to leave. On my last day, I hung up my apron and emptied my pockets of extra guest check pads and pens. I collected my last paycheck and walked out front to say goodbye to Annie Faye who was, of course, seated at the cash register.

"Good thing you're quitting. You near 'bout ate up all my profits," she said. "We used to wonder where you put it all. I never seen anybody your size could eat like that."

Oh, what I would give for that seventeen-year-old metabolism now as I sit, puffy and round and owl-like in my office chair. I had taken a fair amount of teasing for my mounded-up plates at the end of a shift, but I didn't care. Norris's cooked the vegetables with savory ham hocks. The baked potatoes (only available after 5 p.m. and therefore exotic) were crisp on the outside in a way that I have never been able to duplicate. Even the calf's liver was tender and crispy with its standard accompaniment of bacon and mashed potatoes.

After school, I stayed in Wallace to work at the local newspaper and, for many years, ended every single workweek with a Friday night trip to the salad bar and a sizzling steak at Norris's. There was always coconut crème pie, amazing in its own right, as was the lemon and the butterscotch and the chocolate . . . but it was the Grape Hull that I waited for all year. And if it was gone by the time I dragged in after a week of covering town board meetings and weddings and fires and wrecks and general small town mayhem, I would nearly cry.

Over the years, I've made Grape Hull Pie a few times but it has never come close to Annie Faye's. And I've even discussed Grape Hull Pie with a few people who professed to be experts. That is, until they told me they used a double crust. Abomination. Covering that filling with pastry instead of mile-high meringue is a mustache on a culinary Mona Lisa to me.

I hadn't seen Danny's son, "Cousin Daniel," in a while but I knew that he would be the most likely source for his grandma's recipe. A historian, teacher, and author with this own publishing company, Daniel was just a tow-headed toddler when I worked at his family's restaurant. Because it's 2016, I messaged him on Facebook, and within a few hours I was happily reading the recipe, which Daniel says his daddy still makes from time to time.

Norris's Restaurant closed in 2002 and, last I heard, had been transformed into the Del Rio Mexican restaurant. Sombreros and piñatas decorate walls that once were home to genuine replica Confederate swords, a bow to Danny's fondness for Civil War memorabilia. I've heard the margaritas are quite tasty but it's hard to imagine likker drinks being served at the same restaurant where generations of Baptists tucked into generous portions of turkey and dressing and mac and cheese and succotash after church. Not sure what Annie Faye would make of that. Then again, if you've survived a fat Yankee toddler breastfeeding in your restaurant, I reckon you can put up with most anything.

Here it is. My favorite pie of all time. A little slice of Eastern North Carolina on a well-worn china plate at a restaurant on the four lane in Wallace, North Carolina.

Annie Faye Norris's Grape Hull Pie

FILLING:

2 pounds muscadine grapes
½ cup water
¼ stick butter
1 cup sugar
2 ounces fresh lemon juice
  pinch of mace
2 tablespoons cornstarch

In a large bowl, use your fist to mash those grape hulls away from their pulp insides. It's violent, but wonderfully so. Let it all out. Surely somebody has done you wrong this week at some point.

Cook the squished hulls and pulp mixture in a saucepan over medium heat until the seeds separate from the pulp. Pour the pulp through a colander and discard the seeds. Return the grapes to the saucepan and add the water. Cook until the hulls are fork-tender. Add butter, sugar, lemon juice, and mace. Add cornstarch, which you have mixed with enough cold water to make it nice and smooth (about 2 or 3 tablespoons). Continue cooking until it's nice and thickened.

Remove from heat.

Pour into 2 unbaked pie shells and bake at 350° for about 45 minutes.

Remove the pies from the oven, and top with meringue made from 4 or 5 egg whites beaten till stiff with a half cup or so of sugar and cream of tartar. Once you've piled that meringue high, put the pies back in the oven and let those meringue peaks get brown under the broiler. Watch closely; you don't want the meringue to burn.

Serve Grape Hull Pie at room temperature or chilled. Tell your children how it's done. They will thank you one day.

CELIA RIVENBARK is the *New York Times* bestselling author of seven humor collections, a former Duke University media fellow, and a syndicated columnist for Tribune Media Services, whose work appears in newspapers across the country. The proudest moment of her life was when she earned enough from her first newspaper job to buy a washer and dryer and neither one of them had to go on the front porch. She wrote the introduction to Eno Publishers' *27 Views of Wilmington*. She lives in Wilmington with her husband, Scott Whisnant, and their daughter, Sophie.

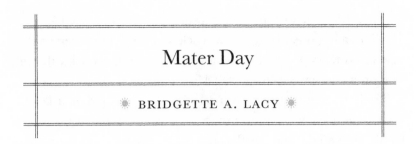

Mater Day

❋ BRIDGETTE A. LACY ❋

IT'S NOT AN official holiday you will find on any calendar. It comes at different times each summer. But Mater Day is a real celebration meant to be shared.

My introduction to this unofficial rite of summer came during my days as a staff writer in the *News & Observer*'s features department. The secretary would send an email announcing the Mater Day potluck.

On one summer day, we came to work armed with all types of tomatoes, mayonnaise, bread, bacon, and lettuce. Folks gathered around the platters of sliced green, red, and yellow beefsteak tomatoes, a feast of color for the eyes.

All afternoon, the staff unabashedly ate their versions of the perfect tomato sandwich. There were those who would slather only Hellmann's on their bread, others Duke's. Some chose white bread, others only wheat. Some liked their tomatoes sliced thin, others thick like meat. No judgments made.

Hours were spent revisiting the makeshift table, the tops of several file cabinets filled with loaves of bread, squeezable jars of mayo, salt and pepper shakers, all the buffet fixings for summer's love apple.

Those juicy, vine-ripe orbs often came directly from someone's backyard, or one of the local farmers markets. Their names were as glorious as their fruit, a sturdy German Johnson, a pretty Mountain Glory, or the yellow and red marbled Ruby Gold.

The seductive smell lured folks for just one more slice, over and over.

When I left the newspaper for a state government job, I kept the festivities alive, organizing my own celebration of the tomato for my new co-workers. I was actually given a plastic badge with the ripe fruit on it and my esteemed title: *Mater Coordinator.*

I took those duties seriously. I asked folks to bring in their favorite variety of the juicy, plump orb. Someone brought the nightshade family's splendid Cherokee Purple, a gorgeous dark mahogany globe of sweetness. Another delivered Brave Boys straight from her garden. Someone else brought in a few German Johnsons from the state farmers market.

It happened again, a lazy, luxurious afternoon of eating tomatoes, marking the ritual of summer that takes us back to our childhoods.

I have to admit, my appreciation for the tomato came with maturity. As a young girl, I ate them on a sandwich with cheese and lettuce. But when my Papa would load my parents up with them during a visit, I sometimes used them as weapons. They made for a great ball of juiciness to throw and watch splatter on the arms and legs of the three brothers who lived across the alley from us. But as I grew into adulthood, it became clear that the love of tomatoes, my genetic heritage, had been passed on to me.

After all, the acidic fruit was a part of my family's DNA.

My earliest memories of tomatoes are from my maternal grandfather's backyard garden. They were one of several prized beauties from his sizeable plot of land. Papa ate tomatoes with everything when they were in season. He sliced them and sprinkled salt and pepper on them and ate them as a side dish. They adorned the buns of grilled burgers and lunch sandwiches.

My mother and her siblings loved to eat them straight off the vine, raw and warm. My mother's sister, Aunt Barbara Anne, recalls wiping the mater on her cotton shorts to get rid of the earth still clinging to it. She often came to the garden with the salt shaker in her hand.

"My daddy's tomato was sweeter than any peach," she recalls. "The juice would run down your arm."

Papa grew Big Boys and later Better Boys. One slice of that big mater would cover almost an entire slice of bread, making it perfect for a sandwich with several slices of the meaty tomato along with thin slices of onion, salt, and pepper between two slices of Sunbeam bread.

When I was growing up, my parents relished a summer breakfast of bacon, fried corn, and sliced tomatoes. I could eat that anytime of the day, and still can.

But probably my favorite way to eat a mater is a BLT. I coat the bread with Hellmann's mayonnaise, add a few large Boston lettuce leaves, several pieces of fried, thick-sliced bacon, and cover the white bread with a few thin, uniform slices of red, purple, and yellow tomatoes seasoned with salt and pepper. I like mixing a few varieties of tomatoes together.

The magic happens when the sliced tomato meets with the generous layer of mayonnaise on the bread. Then I bite down and let the juice run down my arm if I'm lucky. In that moment, I am transported to another time and place, where there are no problems that another bite of that BLT won't make better.

But tomatoes, the quintessential fruit of any garden, shouldn't be eaten alone. So as summer approaches, I am keeping a watchful eye for Mater Day. I browse the various local farmers markets, waiting to see the medley of tomatoes appear on their stands. I can't wait to sound the alarm and send out invitations. The first good tomato sandwich of the summer is cause for a celebration. After all, Mater Day is more than a sandwich.

BRIDGETTE A. LACY is the author of *Sunday Dinner*, a Pat Conroy Cookbook Prize finalist. She is a former feature writer for the *News & Observer* and was the recipient of a North Carolina Arts Fellowship. Her short story, "Lilly's Hunger," was published in *Streetlights: Illuminating Tales of the Urban Black Experience*. Her work has appeared in the *Washington Post, Newsweek,* and *Southern Living.*

Mama Dip's

A Celebration of Southern Food and Music

☀ WILLIAM FERRIS ☀

FOOD AND STRONG Southern women have always played an important part of my life. Before moving to Chapel Hill, I lived in Oxford, Mississippi, where I directed the Center for Study of Southern Culture at the University of Mississippi for eighteen years. My days there often began with breakfast at Smitty's, a restaurant just off the Square run by Louise Smith. Mrs. Smith always greeted me with hot coffee, a plate of steaming biscuits, and homemade preserves.

Sometimes I was joined by my friend Motee Daniels, a bootlegger who sold moonshine to William Faulkner during Prohibition. When Mrs. Smith asked, "What would you like, Motee?" he always replied, "All I need is some kind words and a cool drink of water."

In the evening, I would often drive to the outskirts of Oxford and up a hill to Isaiah's Busy Bee, a small, two-room restaurant with three tables in the front room and a kitchen in the back run by Georgia Isaiah. Mrs. Isaiah had cooked for several chancellors at the University of Mississippi and was renowned for her culinary skills. She prepared one meal with ice tea and a delicious dessert each evening. While I ate, Mrs. Isaiah would lean across the counter and tell me all the news from Oxford.

When my wife, Marcie, and I moved to Chapel Hill in 2002, we enjoyed the celebrated foods prepared by Bill Smith at Crook's Corner and by Ben and Karen Barker at Magnolia Grill. But I also longed for a Southern cuisine in Chapel Hill that would connect me with Louise Smith and Georgia Isaiah's food that I knew and so loved in Oxford.

We quickly made that connection when we met Mildred "Dip" Council and enjoyed a breakfast of grits, eggs, and fried green tomatoes with hot biscuits and coffee at her restaurant Mama Dip's. I also enjoyed lunches and dinners of fried chicken livers, baked sweet potatoes, and sweet tea.

But I needed more than just delicious food. I also sought stories to accompany that food, and those stories came in abundance when I spoke with Mildred Council. Sitting in her favorite booth near the entrance of her restaurant, Mrs. Council greets her visitors with a warmth that makes the food complete. Our friendship has grown and deepened over the past fifteen years in ways that have profoundly enriched my life.

When invited by the Southern Foodways Alliance several years ago to speak about Moon Pies at their annual meeting, I asked Mrs. Council if she remembered eating that delicacy. She immediately replied, "I love a Moon Pie. I'd eat one now if I had it. They were a snack thing that they had everywhere, like in the service stations and grocery stores. I remember at first they all had chocolate. They had a chocolate covering. And in the late eighties and nineties they came out with a cream cover. The inside was crispy like a cracker."[1]

Mrs. Council expanded my study of the American South with her wise voice.

Each fall I teach an 8 a.m. course on Southern music that traces the region's music from its roots in Indian music, spirituals, and ballads to country music, blues, and rock and roll. Inspired by Marcie's study of foodways (see "The Big Book of North Carolina Foodways"), I include a final class on Southern music and food. For that class, my students and I gather in the back room of Mama Dip's around tables laden with her delicious breakfast specials. As the stu-

1. William Ferris, "Moon Pies and Memories," *Southern Cultures* (Summer 2013), 96.

dents begin their breakfast, I lecture about the importance of food in Southern music. Whether at Sacred Harp sings with dinner on the church grounds, at blues house parties, at country music honky-tonks, or at Southern music festivals, food is an essential ingredient of the music performed.

Mama Dip's begins to rock as we listen to a recording of Blind Boy Fuller singing "I Want Some of Your Pie":

> I'm not jokin' and I'm gonner tell you no lie.
> I want to eat your custard pie.
> You got give me some of it,
> 'Fore you give it all away.

Then we listen to Big Bill Lister's recording of "R.C. Cola and Moon Pie." Standing six feet seven inches tall, Lister billed himself as "the world's tallest singing cowboy," and who would dare question his claim as he sang,

> I may be just a country boy,
> But Brother I get my thrill,
> With an R.C. Cola and a Moon Pie,
> Playing "Mabel on the Hill."

There are many food connections to Chapel Hill music worlds. Local band Southern Culture on the Skids insists that before each concert begins, buckets of fried chicken must be passed out to their audience, who then eat the chicken while dancing to songs with lines like

> Got too much pork for just one fork.
> Won't you pass that apple pie?

Interviewed by my student Michael Spinks, bandleader Rick Miller explains, "Our music is a lot like a Southern plate lunch. Every item on the menu has been cooking for a while and has its own flavor, but they all run together when you put them on the plate and start to eat. We take a lot of different styles—blues, rock, surf, easy listening, country—and let them all run together when we play."[2]

Then I spice up the topic of Southern food and music with Goodie Mob singing "Soul Food."

> Daddy put the hot grits on my chest in the morning.
> When I was sick, Mary had the hot soup boiling.
> Didn't know why, but it felt so good,
> Like some waffles in that morning.
> Headed back to the woods.
> Now I'm full as a tick, got some soul on blast in the cassette.
> Food for my brain. I haven't stopped learning yet.
> Hot wings from mo-jos got my forehead sweating.
> Celery and blue cheese on my menu next.

From blues to country to rock and roll to hip-hop, we sample sounds and explore how they celebrate foodways through music.

Bill Smith generously takes time to join my class and speaks about his work as chef at Crook's Corner. Bill explains that many local musicians have worked as sous chefs in his kitchen to support themselves. Bill also once ran Cat's Cradle, where musicians who worked in his kitchen also performed with their bands. He acknowledges his debt to Mrs. Council, whose work at Mama Dip's is an inspiration for his own.

Then Mrs. Council speaks to the class. She tells students how she received her nickname "Dip" as a young girl because she was tall and could lean over and dip water from the barrel at her home when her siblings were thirsty. Mrs. Council carries us back in time to her life as a child in rural Orange County and her memory of the country store

2. Michael Spinks, "Building Community Through Consumption, Commodification, and Reconsumption via 'White-Trash' Themes and Community Involvement: S.C.O.T.S.—A Case Study of A Band." Term paper in Southern Music (Folklore/History 100), December 17, 2002: pp. 4, 12.

where her father traded eggs and the produce he raised for coffee and supplies the family needed:

> The country store is important. We talk about it all the time, the older generation like me. Today you go to the freezer and take things out. But in the country store nothing was boxed up. The meat was hung in the loft of the store, the ham, and the shoulder and the strick o'lean.
>
> It smelled good because even the candy was laying out. The peppermint sticks weren't wrapped up. The horehound and the Mounds was three times as big as they are today. I remember we swapped eggs in the country for our goodies.
>
> Let me tell you about the country store. Everybody knowed everybody. We would ride to town on a wagon.
>
> People would sit outside, and they could tell time by that shadow. Poppa could too. When dinnertime came, he would say, "Well the bell's gonner ring in a little bit." And that shadow would be real small, you know. Old people could tell the time of day with the shadow. People today don't know about it any more.[3]

Mrs. Council's stories and her delicious breakfast are clearly the highlight of my course on Southern music. Her tales and the taste of her cuisine are memories that my students and I will savor for many years. They are an anchor that is distinctive to Chapel Hill, a city where food and story are forever associated with Mildred Council's powerful culinary voice.

3. William Ferris, "The Moon Pie: A Southern Journey," in *Cornbread Nation: The Best of Southern Food Writing*, ed. Dale Volberg Reed and John Shelton Reed. General editor, John T. Edge (Athens: University of Georgia, 2008), 158-59.

WILLIAM FERRIS is the Joel R. Williamson Eminent Professor of History at the University of North Carolina at Chapel Hill and Senior Associate Director of its Center for the Study of the American South. Former chairman of the National Endowment for the Humanities, he has written or edited thirteen books and created fifteen documentary films. His most recent book is *The South in Color: A Visual Journal.*

The Mesopotamia of Pork

☀ DANIEL H. WALLACE ☀

LEXINGTON, NORTH CAROLINA, is to barbecue what Paris, France, is to baguettes. When I was a kid I imagined everyone in Paris walking around with a baguette or two under their arms, like Little League baseball bats in thin paper sacks. This turned out to be true, sort of, or at the very least *kind* of true: I went to Paris once and I tell you, you have never seen so many baguettes in one place in all your life. They call Paris "The City of Lights" only because they crowd-tested "The City of Baguettes," and it didn't play as well.

But Lexington does in fact call itself "The Barbecue Capital of North Carolina," and not for nothing: With a joint like the Bar-B-Q Center in the city limits you can get away with it. And with an annual barbecue festival that a few years back drew over 200,000 people and had Darius Rucker play for free? Please. Still, it's a gutsy self-appellation: In a state with such a rich barbecue heritage, to call oneself the Barbecue Capital is an audacious claim, especially since the Tar Heel state is split in half by those who prefer one style of barbecue over another. Barbecue doyens may recall that one style is called *Eastern* and that the other is called *Western*, or, more commonly, *Lexington-style*—as in the style of how they do it in Lexington, and how they do it (expertly, I might add) at the Bar-B-Q Center.

The Bar-B-Q Center is one of the best-known barbecue joints— not just in the state—but in the country. It's on Main Street, not far from I-85, on a rise just before heading into town, and if you've been on Main Street in Lexington anytime in the last fifty years or so you know where it is, because it hasn't moved or even changed that much since it got there in 1961, even though everything around it has. There's a storage center across the street, and an automotive center nearby too, but they're babies to the neighborhood compared to the Bar-B-Q Center.

What a joint this is. Even vegetarians should give it a visit. There are places in the world that feel as if they've been passed over by the dulling effects of time, rescued from the past for presentation in the present. The Bar-B-Q Center is a place like this. Its iconic neon sign should be sheltered in the Smithsonian one day, next to Julia Child's kitchen. The red-brick and cinder-block building is sturdy, perfect in its simplicity. A wolf could huff and puff and never blow it down. The pigs cowering within would be entirely safe.

It's not a big place. The restaurant seats approximately a hundred. But even when it's full it doesn't feel crowded—probably because there are so many booths. There's something about snagging a seat in a big comfortable booth that makes a body feel taken care of. There's a long row of red vinyl-covered stools along the counter where the solitary can sit. Here you can watch the large-screen television mounted near the ceiling, or gawk in wonder as half a dozen waiters and waitresses and cooks artfully negotiate a space not much wider than a balancing beam. One waitress I interviewed on deep background did admit that it was tight back there and occasionally you might have a friendly collision or two, and then she filled up my diet soda.

The Bar-B-Q Center has been owned and operated by the same family since 1961. It started out as an ice cream store, but one winter, when ice cream sales took a dip, they put a shoulder on a pit and the rest is history. They still sell lots of ice cream—around 200 gallons a week, much of it going into a ridiculously huge 3.5-pound banana split, which this intrepid reporter was not intrepid enough to eat.

Sonny and Nancy Conrad ran the center for decades, until Sonny died some years ago. Nancy still works, but the day-to-day running of the business falls to her sons, Michael and Cecil. In an online posting, Michael Conrad writes that he sees barbecue as being one of the few remaining professions where knowledge is passed down from mentor to apprentice, over time, through direct experience. You can't learn to cook barbecue, he argues: You have to live it, and from what I've learned as a self-anointed barbecue critic, I think this is the truth. The pit-masters I've met haven't just taken it up as a hobby or a second career: It's been a part of their lives in one way or another from the get-go.

But Cecil did get out of the business for a while. He went away for five years and got his masters in sports medicine. He says he always knew he'd come back one day, even though his father never pushed him to—"He nudged," Cecil says. The only big change Cecil and Michael brought to the joint happened recently, when they replaced the original pits with new ones, expanding the kitchen. The new pits are beautiful, airtight; the hot orange coals glow like a thousand setting suns. And the pork shoulders that come out of them are tender; the meat falls off the bone. You need to experience barbecue straight from the pit cooked by a pro—it's like tasting spring, though it's still great when it gets to the table. It's moist, tomato-y, a little smoky. Follow it with the red slaw for a superior barbecue experience.

* * *

IN THE SIXTIES, Main Street in Lexington was a popular place to cruise, so the center had a very popular curb service. The hot rods used the parking lot as a turnaround, and rode back and forth down Main Street all night long. Sonny tired of it, though, and installed a metal railing to keep the ducktails out. He had nothing against them but he knew, with the wisdom displayed by barbecue's early settlers, that he wanted his to be a family business, and that's exactly what he got. And they still have curb service.

So, the Barbecue Capital of North Carolina? I'd go even further. I'd say Lexington is the Mesopotamia of North Carolina barbecue. Not that barbecue was born here, or invented here, or that without it we wouldn't know what to do with a pit of hot coals and a pork shoulder. Good barbecue is everywhere. But there is something similar about the North Carolina Piedmont and the fertile crescent of the Tigris and Euphrates river basin: Civilization comes from one, and barbecue comes from the other.

DANIEL WALLACE has written five novels, including *Big Fish*, and a children's book; his sixth novel, *Extraordinary Adventures*, will be published in Spring 2017. His work has been translated into twenty-five languages, and his essays and illustrations have appeared in many magazines, including *Vanity Fair* (in Italy) and *Garden & Gun*, where he is a contributing editor. He is the J. Ross MacDonald Distinguished Professor of English at the University of North Carolina at Chapel Hill, and is married to Laura Kellison Wallace.

Hard Crab Stew

☀ BILL SMITH ☀

ONCE, I WAS driving from New Bern to Cedar Island with a carful of siblings and a friend from the West Coast. When we began crossing the wetlands after Beaufort, a familiar aroma filled the car. Tidal marsh. "I love that smell!" I exclaimed in unison with my brother and sister. Silence from our guest. An acquired taste, I suppose, if you didn't grow up on the coast. Happily, I did grow up there. My great-grandmother was the daughter of a lighthouse keeper, in fact. All kinds of customs and rituals from the Outer Banks informed our childhood even though the family had moved inland during the Depression. Hard Crab Stew is the dinner I think of first when I think of home.

There are several reasons why a Hard Crab Stew dinner was always a special occasion. As likely as not we would be cooking it at the beach, and we would have caught and cleaned all of the crabs ourselves. Because it is messy to eat, it would be served at long, newspaper-covered tables outside. Lastly, even if it weren't so messy, this type of stew is a fair amount of trouble, so it doesn't turn up often or without planning. My grandmother, an instinctive cook, was the Queen of Crab Stew. It was literally years of trying before I could produce one worthy of comparison with hers. And this only after an alternative version (in her handwriting!) turned up in the recipe box of a neighbor.

When I was growing up, crabs were free food. They are ridiculously easy to catch. Everybody had a crab net. The only other things you needed were some string and a few chicken necks. Early morning was the best time. Sunset was next. You had to try not to scare them with your shadow. They can't resist the chicken necks (or fish guts) that you dangle before them. Even if they escape your net the first time, they come right back. A couple of dozen and you have stew.

Learning to clean them was problematic because they will pinch you if they can and because early on I didn't want to hurt them. I'm over that now and not because I was assured by everyone that "they can't feel it." I didn't believe that then and I don't believe it now. Today it seems that I am the only person who remembers how to clean crabs at all. People vanish when it's time to take on this task. It's best done outside and it usually involves beer, a garden hose, and mosquitos.

The dish is full of crab and potatoes, but even so, it's the broth that makes the stew. It is salty with fatback and thickened with cornmeal. It saturates the sliced white bread used to line its bowl. Crabs are cleaned, snapped in half, and stewed in their shells. The seasoning is simple: red pepper flakes, thyme, and a bay leaf or two. Big pieces of potato are cooked with the crabs.

It is eaten with the hands as much as with a spoon, and it is impossible to eat Hard Crab Stew with any sort of table manners. This is why we are all sitting outside. Hands and nutcrackers are the way to go. Piles of shells begin to collect among the soup bowls. Unseemly noises are heard coming from the diners. People are scolded for cracking crab shells with their teeth.

With any luck we're sitting on the deck of a cottage somewhere out on Hatteras Island. Late in the afternoon there comes a moment when the sun is still hot, but the wind starts to come in off the sea. Heat radiates up from the sand as the breeze cools you at the same time. When this happens, tension magically leaves my neck and shoulders for a second. I feel like I am where I belong.

"You could live here," I think to myself, but actually, no I can't. Life's obligations have taken me elsewhere. So instead, for a minute or two, I am grateful for the good luck that allows me to return there from time to time and for the memories these visits provide.

Hard Crab Stew

SERVES A CROWD

½ pound sidemeat or fatback
2 medium onions, cut into large dice
2 dozen hard crabs, cleaned and halved
½ teaspoon crushed red pepper flakes
4 bay leaves
1 teaspoon dried thyme
6 baking potatoes, peeled and cut into eighths
¾ cup all-purpose cornmeal, or better yet, Maseca,
  stirred into 2 cups of cold water until smooth
  Salt and pepper to taste
  Sliced white bread

Render the sidemeat in a large stockpot on low heat. It smokes at a low temperature. Cook until brown and crispy. Add onions and sauté until soft but not brown. Add the crabs, pepper flakes, bay leaves, thyme, and cover with cold water. Bring to a boil, reduce the heat and simmer for half an hour.

Add the potatoes and cook until they are well done, 15 to 20 minutes more. Turn up the heat a little and stir in the cornmeal and water. Mix thoroughly. Turn back down to a simmer and cook until the stew begins to thicken. Season with salt and pepper.

Place pieces of bread in the bottom of soup bowls and ladle the stew over the top.

BILL SMITH is the chef of Chapel Hill's famous Crook's Corner. He has twice been a finalist for the James Beard Award for Best Chef in the Southeast. He is the author of *Seasoned in the South* and, most recently, *Crabs and Oysters*. He is a contributor to Eno Publishers' *27 Views of Chapel Hill*.

The Crab King

JEFFERY BEAM

For Patricia Owens, Mary Frances Vogler, Stanley Finch
New Bern, Independence Day 1999

It's not greed
         that demands I should catch you,

but the Goddess
         who decrees
         that we should eat,
                that each of us
at one time, or another, under the silver sun
will give up the self so
         another might live.

You out-foxed me again and again—
sleazy pig tails
         sullying the water
with their salts,
         one feather floating above you
         offered as a barge.

What can I give you as fair exchange?

Eye for eye?
            Tooth for tooth? Or
simply praise-song in these words
                              which sacrifice, too,
                              sayeth the Lord,

as my body continues browning under summer's lamp,

and the light goes out in you,
                        entering me
                              with atoning claws?

My promise? To live!
                  Live!

No longer crawling along the dirty-sanded bottom,
but up in the light,

                  where the skin peels.
                  Where the spirit has a house.

JEFFERY BEAM is a poet, singer, editor, and photographer. His books of poetry include *Gospel Earth, The New Beautiful Tendons, Visions of Dame Kind, The Broken Flower,* and *An Elizabethan Bestiary.* He is the creator of the spoken-word collection, *What We Have Lost: New and Selected Poems, 1977–2001.* His next book is *Spectral Pegasus / Dark Movements,* a collaboration with Welsh painter Clive Hicks-Jenkins. Born and raised in Kannapolis, he has lived in Hillsborough since 1975.

Putting on the Grits

✴ MORETON NEAL ✴

"WHAT ARE GRITS?"

I couldn't help overhearing this query from a well-dressed young woman sitting at the table next to me at one of Asheville's most popular breakfast spots, Tupelo Honey. The waitress had to stop and think about the answer, which gave me the opportunity to butt into the conversation.

The poor customer didn't know what hit her. How could she have known she was sitting next to the former wife of Bill Neal, the late author of *Good Old Grits*? This is the same man who in the Eighties re-invented Shrimp and Grits, transforming a simple breakfast dish to one of the most requested main courses in the South . . . with the exception, apparently, of Florida where the woman happened to live. (Her grits ignorance proves the old cliché, Florida really isn't a Southern state at all.)

Needless to say, she now knows more than she ever wanted to about grits.

She can report back to the uninitiated in her home state that grits sustained Native Americans for thousands of years . . . that the Aztecs are credited with the invention of hominy (corn kernels soaked in lye water to remove the husk) . . . that after drying, hominy was ground into meal, cooked with water, and the result was not unlike the food made from cooking ground barley with water that sustained Old World masses for millennia: gruel. We Americans call our version *grits*.

The Floridian also knows that corn was introduced to Europe by

Venetian traders in the sixteenth century . . . that the plant thrived in Italian soil . . . that its ground meal eventually replaced barley in making gruel. The result is polenta, a staple of Italian cuisine.

So, basically, if you know polenta, you know grits, and vice versa. Nowadays grits—at least the stoneground version now popular in contemporary Southern cuisine—are usually made from dried white or yellow corn rather than lye-soaked hominy, which means the only real difference between grits and polenta is size: Polenta is quite finely ground; grits are grittier.

After this unsolicited crash course in grits, the Asheville tourist, feeling just a teeny bit under the gun, did forego hash browns and made the correct choice—grits with her eggs and sausage.

She may not repeat the experience. The grits that day were pretty good, but nothing to write home about, though the waitress assured us they were stoneground. Even with the added texture and flavor enhanced by grinding them with stone rather than steel, grits (like rice and pasta) play a supporting role to other ingredients. The right amount of salt is essential, and good fresh butter, of course. The cooking liquid is important—grits improve when cooked with chicken stock, milk, or cream (or all of the above) instead of plain water.

But even when cooked to perfection, grits demand company. Sausage, ham, or bacon, and fresh eggs (preferably fried, with runny yolks) create the synergy that results in a satisfying meal. Red-eye or sausage gravy ice the cake, so to speak. Unfortunately for the novitiate from the Sunshine State, we left the restaurant before giving her full instructions on the wide world of grits pairing and grits preparing.

Some Southerners gussy up their grits with cheese and bind them with eggs. This combination (often with garlic, Tabasco, and nutmeg added) produces a dish variously called baked cheese grits, cheese grits soufflé, or grits casserole. Whatever the name, it usually means company is expected for breakfast or brunch.

If you would rather someone else cook your grits, you don't have to go far, particularly here in the Triangle. Since Bill Neal introduced his version of shrimp and grits at Crook's Corner in 1983, I daresay this dish has become the most popular restaurant meal, not only at Crook's, but also in regional restaurants all over the South (except Florida, I guess). Charleston—where it is impossible to find a restaurant that doesn't serve its own variation of the dish—may have gained the title of shrimp-and-grits capital of the world. But those Charlestonians can have the world title. Our Raleigh/Durham/Chapel Hill chefs make the best grits on the planet.

Baked Cheese Grits

SERVES 6 TO 8

4   cups whole milk
1   cup stoneground grits
½   teaspoon salt
½   cup butter
4   eggs
2   cups grated sharp cheddar
1   clove crushed garlic (optional)
    a dash of Tabasco and Worcestershire sauces (optional)

Bring the milk to a simmer in a medium-sized saucepan. Slowly pour in the grits while stirring. Add salt and continue to cook over low heat for 40 minutes to an hour, depending on package instructions. Stir frequently.

When grits are done, stir in the butter, eggs, cheese, and garlic and sauces, if using. Pour into a greased 2-quart casserole dish. Bake in a 350° oven for 30 minutes or up to an hour, depending on the depth of the dish. The middle should be firm to the touch.

For variations, substitute Parmesan for some of the cheddar or use Gruyère, not a Southern flavor but delicious with lamb or roast chicken.

Before she became an interior designer, MORETON NEAL was a pastry chef, restaurateur, food editor, restaurant reviewer, culinary-talk-show host, and cookbook author. Her column, *Joyous Cooking*, is a regular feature of *Chapel Hill Magazine*. She still enjoys cooking for her husband, friends, children, and grandchildren at home in Chapel Hill.

ADVENTURES IN EATING

Vulnerability

❋ SOPHIA WOO ❋

VULNERABILITY. OF ALL the emotions that have coursed through me during my journey with food I keep coming back to that terrifying and exhilarating state of being. Teetering on the edge of success and failure, I've taken the plunge and exposed myself. Will they like me? Will I fail miserably? Will I still be standing tomorrow? Honestly, I'm not a chef. I'm not an entrepreneur by nature. I'm not even good at taking risks because being vulnerable isn't something I find comfortable. So how did I get to this point?

Even before entering the food world, I found food interesting. Depending on context and situation, food can be a need or a want or a downright luxury. It can be the foundation of good health, a way to learn about a new culture, or a way to celebrate those highest moments in life. We eat our way through first dates, through travel to new places, through religious experiences, and even through boredom. Food is our way to connect to our surroundings and connect with people.

Growing up I spent every summer in Taiwan, where my extended family lived. As I grew older I noticed that I increasingly missed the food between trips. It went from sporadic cravings, to near obsessions that led to quests for comparable food in North Carolina and scouring the Internet for recipes when that failed. And of course, the eateries I insisted on visiting each trip were the ones that served food that had reached cultural status. You know, the food that's dripping with history, that has been made the same way for years and years, and that every grandmother possessed her own secret family recipe—*that* kind of food. There's the small shop that sells *shui jian boa* (crispy pan fried and steamed buns) filled with Chinese leeks and dried shrimp that has sold out every day for over twenty-five years. There's the noodle shop selling vermicelli in a thick fragrant soup with oysters and pig intestines that has no open seats so everyone, including the businesspeople in suits, just squats and slurps. There's the sweet sticky rice with a dried longan on top sold by little old ladies in visors outside of temples that I could only eat after presenting it as an offering and bowing three times to the temple gods.

It was this kind of food that first made me want to cook and share. It was this kind of food that just made me feel bad my American friends weren't experiencing it. Food so good, you get upset if you can't have it every day and you pity others who've never tasted it. I think that's what drives me when it comes to food—wanting everyone to have a dish so good, they're jealous of themselves while eating it. More than fresh ingredients, food trends, and beautiful presentation, what I most want to share is that momentary euphoria. But could I get it right?

At first it was just a plan. Sunny, my business partner, and I both wanted something new and exciting and our own. Then, we found a $7000 truck on craigslist. Then, it was a Kickstarter pledge drive where we told the world our dreams and I just hoped we wouldn't be laughed at. Then, it was amazing support from all over North Carolina. Then, the surreal moment of winning a national television contest. That happened in only two years, but when we tell the short version of our story, we gloss over the day-to-day grind and the moments of intense vulnerability.

The first year of business, rolling around Raleigh as the Dump Pho King Truck (our name before the Food Network had us change it to Pho Nomenal Dumpling Truck), was tough—full of worst-case scenarios and barely making it to the next day. Pipes burst, water heaters broke, screens ripped, inspections were terrifying. And the whole time we were trying desperately to cook up to expectations and look put-together in front of customers.

I remember the second time our engine broke, Sunny and I just sat by the side of the road, waiting for the tow truck. She turned to me with tears in her eyes and asked me if I thought this was a sign that we just weren't meant to do this. I didn't answer right away because I really didn't know. That first year wasn't triumphant. It was hard work every day and it showed in our bodies. We suffered from constant heat rash, weight loss, dehydration, and intense bouts of frustration. What made it worth it was people came to eat. I can't tell you how much it meant when someone came back to the truck to compliment us and chat about the food and the business.

I distinctly remember one older gentleman who returned to the truck and commented that he had served in Vietnam and the only thing that would make our pho more authentic would be the smell of jet fuel in the air.

We had just survived our first year when the Food Network cold-called us about auditioning for *The Great Food Truck Race,* a reality road-trip competition that pits food trucks from around the country against each other. Sunny said, "What's the worst that could happen?" "Well," I responded, "something could happen to the truck, or even worse—we could fail on national television." Images of past reality-TV meltdowns flashed through my head, and I thought about all the awful memes and hashtags that could arise. Surely, no amount of airtime is worth that. But Sunny has taught me not to be afraid, to forge into the unknown, to ask for help if we get stuck. It might put us in a vulnerable position, but we can always figure it out as we go.

So we said yes. Our newly renamed Pho Nomenal Dumpling Truck did break down on national television and we did have very public failures. We broke down on our way to our first location, right in the middle of the busiest road in Lake Havasu, Arizona. All I saw in our rear-view mirror was a huge plume of smoke rising from the back of the truck, as our camera operator exclaimed, "Oh shit. Is this story?"

Somehow we came alive in the chaos. The experience we'd had with all the breakdowns and bumps that first year of business, including our other massive engine failure, became helpful. With everyone safely out of the truck, I immediately got on the phone looking for a tow truck. We had been towed to events before, and while it sucked, it wouldn't necessarily spell the end. As a testament to our shared experience, Sunny had the exact same idea and we tied up a tow company's phone line, calling them at the same time.

The police and the fire department arrived, too, and our production team got fantastic shots of this breaking story. When the tow truck arrived, one problem was solved, but as the weekend went on our luck continued to worsen. We had to be towed everywhere (which cost money); our week-old generator broke, so we had to rent one (more money); and our propane tank malfunctioned and we ran out of propane, leaving us with only our electrical power devices to cook. We kept cooking and hustling, hoping that our dumplings and fun Asian food would bring us crowds. We got as creative strategy-wise as we could, but physical exhaustion, heat (it was over 90 degrees *outside* the truck), and stress took their toll. In spite of the setbacks, Sunny was already petitioning our director to bring us back for the show's all-star/second-chance season.

Had we broken down in any city other than Lake Havasu we wouldn't have lasted the weekend. But we were in a city that cared. Word spread fast and people came. They waited for us, they followed us, they devoured our food, they tried to help in every way they could, and they gave us smiles and words of encouragement. Against all odds we came through. And though I promised myself that I would not cry on national television, I teared up during the show's elimination round, coming precariously close to ruining my makeup, which would have been perfect considering the very real possibility that it could have been our last moment in the spotlight. But we had more moments in the spotlight—lots of mistakes, some triumphs, periods of vulnerability, all captured on video and aired to the world.

Despite our many setbacks, Pho Nomenal Dumpling Truck returned to Raleigh as the winner of *The Great Food Truck Race.*

＊　＊　＊

SO WHAT AM I, if not a chef or an entrepreneur? I am a person who is stubborn, who loves pho, and who works at whatever I'm doing, relentlessly. Through all this I've learned if you ever get to the point where you aren't feeling vulnerable when you tell someone your dreams or serve them a dish, you aren't dreaming big enough.

SOPHIA WOO graduated from the University of North Carolina's Kenan-Flagler Business School with a business administration degree and a masters in accounting. She and her business partner launched Raleigh-based Pho Nomenal Dumpling Truck in 2014. They have been serving up traditional Asian recipes with a twist ever since and have built a loyal fan base. They were nationally recognized when they took home first place and a $50,000 grand prize in the Food Network's *The Great Food Truck Race*.

Orange You Glad

* EMILY WALLACE *

SOMEWHERE BETWEEN THE point I learned to ride a bike and the year I saved enough money to buy a pair of rollerblades, I gained permission to drive the riding lawnmower down the driveway and around the road's bend to my uncle's house—a .2-mile blip that stretched forever when using the mower's "turtle" speed setting. My uncle and dad co-owned a farm equipment store in Smithfield— inherited from their father and their father's father, who started the thing as a mule company in the Thirties. This was something of the family tradition, the preferred mode of transportation. I have a framed photograph of my dad atop a Model B tractor, about the age I was on my maiden mower voyage. And though the picture is black and white, I know the tractor was orange: the signature hue for both the Allis-Chalmers and Kubota rigs we sold.

In the rural world there are John Deere families, and New Holland families, and Farmall families, and Massey Ferguson families. But we were solidly an Allis-Chalmers and Kubota family because *we* were an orange family, one sustained on the likes of pimento cheese, cheese puffs, and Cheez-Its. That's not to say we didn't eat our vege-tables. My dad kept a garden in the backyard and my mother swears (and photographs concur) that I ate so many carrots as a kid the tip of my nose turned a bright shade of tangerine. But when we did eat our greens, we often (and I always) covered them with a sheath of American cheese.

The real crux of orange living, however, is the Nab—a simple combination of two cheese crackers and a smear of peanut butter

–88–

that takes its nickname from Nabisco, which manufactured an early line of the snack, but was made by multiple brands. I don't recall the first time I had one, but I'm fairly certain where it came from: the storage room of my dad's shop. Prior to its life as a farm store, the building was a prison camp on the edge of town, and the back room was the last relic of that space, with iron bars shading its windows. On one wall of the room, a Lance brand vending machine was tightly guarded, too, with lesser bars blocking its signature Toast-Chee crackers. I used to linger by my dad's side at work, hopeful for a handful of dimes to spend on them. When successful, I shared the snack with Dot, the secretary whose name I spelled as a large, dark circle on a page.

Then the business closed. The national farming crisis of the 1980s was bad for selling tractors; farmers didn't have funds for shiny new orange equipment. But they likely had money for a cheap pack of Nabs; the sandwich crackers have been recession food from the beginning. In 1928, on the verge of the Great Depression, Karlie Keith Fisher built a company in the basement of her Raleigh home combining plain crackers and peanut butter. The enterprise was so successful she eventually expanded her line of products and moved into a larger space, with the Fisher/Rex brand operating well into the 1990s. Similarly, using the peanuts with which Philip Lance launched his Charlotte-based company in 1913, Mary Lance and their two daughters began making sandwich crackers in 1915, logging their first million-dollar year of sales in 1935. Three years later, the economy still slumping, they introduced their own ToastChee variety.

Like its hardtack forebears, the ToastChee became a staple of the country store. And as the South increasingly industrialized, it hopped onto dope carts—wagons that wheeled through textile mills and sold "dopes" (colas) and snacks to workers who were forced to eat on the job as they found time—and settled into vending machines, where its crisp orange shell shone behind paned glass like a neon vacancy sign.

Nabs were, and still are, the king of a road trip, the salve on a workday. After my dad and his brother closed the business and auctioned off the last bits of farm equipment, he took a job as a traveling salesman, driving all over the eastern part of the state to sell industrial parts to shops including farm equipment stores. As such, his car was something of a souped-up supply closet crammed with samples to show customers—gadgets and goods that could also solve any problem encountered on the road. There were trays of nuts and bolts in the trunk, a suitcase crammed with glues (including a spacey sounding epoxy called E-6000) in the backseat, a floorboard lined with solvents, and a console stocked with Nabs (on special days there were Rolo chocolates, too).

As a writer and folklorist, I've driven my fair share of the state to conduct fieldwork. And like my dad, I've driven many of those miles with Nabs at my side—or, at least, at the roadside. But on a recent boat trip, I made a misstep, traveling without them. It was Homecoming Day for Portsmouth Island—a wild and gorgeous speck on the Outer Banks that served as a major port and lifesaving station until a string of hurricanes helped shift those industries elsewhere. Residents followed that work up-shore until the population eventually declined from nearly 700 folks in 1860 to just three, and later zero, in 1971. Descendants of the island return every other year for the big Homecoming event, which includes a hymn-sing in the old Methodist Church and a dinner on the grounds. They lug coolers of deviled eggs and sodas, platters of baked ham and fried chicken, and boxes of pies and cakes all by boat from Ocracoke Island—some 5.5 miles across the Ocracoke Inlet, and another twenty or so more via ferry from the mainland.

Accompanying a fellow writer on assignment, I climbed into an open fishing boat wearing flip-flops, a thin shirt, and a thinner rain jacket around 7 a.m., expecting the sun to eventually burn off the early morning mist. Instead, more clouds came in. Under a pitched tent—one intended to block the sun—the main program commenced with praise for the day's perfect weather. Yes, it was unseasonably cold for late April, admitted the Friends of Portsmouth's president, but the cool temps and constant wind were keeping the island's notorious mosquitoes at bay.

I know, I know, it's not like I was faced with the hurricane of 1846. But having skipped breakfast and no longer able to feel my fingertips, I was ready to abandon the little island for home. The Gilgos, Salters, Pigotts, and other surnames announced during the family roll call portion of the ceremony were clearly stronger and more resilient than I. We obviously weren't cut from the same cloth. Then I heard something that rang familiar and familial. "Would you like a Nab?" the voice asked, handing me two. And I settled into Homecoming suddenly sure of something: When Faulkner described his "postage stamp of native soil," he must have meant the notch-edged Nab.

EMILY WALLACE is a writer and illustrator based in Durham. Her work has appeared in numerous publications including the *Washington Post*, *Southern Living*, *Our State*, and *Gravy*. She is deputy editor of *Southern Cultures* quarterly.

Pie Love You, Cake Do Without You

✻ MARIANNE GINGHER ✻

IN THE BEGINNING, he acted like a man who hadn't eaten a home-cooked meal in twenty years. He told me that his first wife had been too unhappy to cook and the second one, too angry. He couldn't get over my cooking. He didn't cook, but he'd sit in the kitchen and watch me frying up chicken livers or making Lowcountry crab cakes out of a Charleston cookbook or rolling out a pie crust, and his handsome face wore the balmiest, most satisfied look that I'd ever seen on a man. I'd grown up among Southern cooks: My maternal grandmother, a slow and dreamy cook, was from Kentucky and my paternal grandmother from North Carolina. They knew their way around the Southern kitchen, and I have their recipes to prove it—though I never saw either of them consult a cookbook. My Kentucky grandmother, Elizabeth, made a twelve-egg angel food cake from scratch that was as tender as fluff and always accompanied by cups of boiled vanilla custard, served chilled, that you dipped slices of the cake into. Her mother, my great-grandmother Mary Yeager, had taught her to churn butter, and Granny had much respect for butter. You never spread anything *but* on your toast or the yeast-risen bran rolls she baked when you visited her. Granny was a superb pie maker. Her signature dessert was a fairy-tale concoction called Coronation Butterscotch Pie made with caramelized sugar and slathered with turrets of meringue. She loved to tell the story about that pie saving her marriage.

My North Carolina grandmother, Ruth, a jackrabbit in the kitchen, made cakes more than she baked pies. She served a killer skillet cornbread and deep-fried her own hush puppies. Both my grandmothers fried chicken up a storm. In the summer Grandmother Ruth stirred up the sweetest succotash I've ever eaten, a toss of garden fresh baby lima beans and Silver Queen corn, the kernels as tiny and white as baby teeth with lots of fresh black pepper and just the right amount of bacon fat. We sprinkled vinegar and sugar on our sliced German Johnson tomatoes, and she made a watermelon rind pickle so luminous and translucent green it could have come from the Emerald City of Oz.

My mother loved to bake pies, and my first cooking lesson, when I was ten or so, was learning how to make a pie crust. The only pie I didn't try to bake was the Coronation Butterscotch Pie. Its history intimidated me, but Mother was a whiz at it. Only after she stopped cooking did I give it a go, much to my sons' delight, and for all the trouble it is to make, it's become a holiday staple.

Today, I'm a big fan of *The Moosewood Cookbook*, Laurie Colwin's *Home Cooking*, *The Silver Palate*, and the many recipes offered by Melissa Clark and Mark Bittman that I've clipped from the *New York Times*. But my most cherished recipe book, the one I'd grab first if my kitchen caught on fire, is my tattered copy of Marion Flexner's 1949 *Out of Kentucky Kitchens*. The plain dusty color of a russet potato, it belonged to my mother. Before I read the preface by Duncan Heinz, I thought Duncan Heinz was only a brand of cake mix. He was a traveling salesman from Bowling Green, Kentucky, who accidentally became a restaurant critic. He and his wife put together a popular book about his gastronomical pit stops while on the road, called *Adventures in Good Eating*. Later, he wrote a syndicated column about eateries he'd visited nationwide. "I'm not a professional cook myself, but I do know good cooking. . . . All good cooks give to each dish the loving care that it needs," he writes in the preface.

I happen to believe that you can taste "loving care" if foods are truly prepared with it, and it pleases me to have corroboration from an expert taster. In my mind, the essence of "loving care" is unrushed, small-batch cooking for people you truly like and want to please. When folks asked Duncan Heinz where the best place to eat was, he always replied, "In your own home."

❋   ❋   ❋

BUT BACK TO my man and how he loved to eat what I cooked—and I cooked slow, jackrabbit, and *loud*. I daydreamed and hummed. Then I hurried. I dropped things, cut myself with a paring knife and hollered, splashed around in the sink, rattling pans, made a mess like Julia Child. The chicken would be sputtering in the skillet, the radio playing, my man would jump off his stool and twirl me around, then I'd flip a drumstick. Years later, I would run across an article somebody had clipped from the *Greensboro Daily News* back when I was growing up in the late 1960s. It was from a local advice column and was titled, "Why Grow Old Alone? Here's Your Chance to Learn Men's Likes in Women." The following quotes are from the men who were surveyed:

> We like women who are good company, but dislike one who is loud. We love that soft, feminine voice. . . . A loud voice is good for a hog caller, but not for a woman who wants to appeal to men. . . . . Give us gentle women who think of us as kings, thus inspiring us to respond with the love and loyalty due a queen.

> In our little love-nest kitchen, my king treated me like I was a queen, though I whooped like a hog caller and danced until the buzzer went off. Then I slid an old-fashioned chocolate cream pie out of the oven or a hot milk cake to be iced with "Carrie Byck's Double Fudge Frosting" from my *Kentucky Kitchens* cookbook.

"Pie love you," my man said. "Cake do without you."

He really and truly talked like that.

❋   ❋   ❋

JUST ABOUT THE only Southern cooking I wasn't halfway good at was making biscuits, and now and again my man loved a good Southern biscuit.

Some days for lunch, we'd cruise down the long East Franklin Street hill to a little hole-in-the-wall drive-thru called Sunrise Biscuit Kitchen and buy chicken sandwiches with pickles, mayo, and mustard. The folks at the Sunrise made a big fluffy biscuit, tender in the center, but with crunch on the top. The chicken was fried. Not as peppery as my grandmothers made theirs, but just as tender, juicy, not overly salted, and crisp. My man sometimes liked his with coleslaw.

I'd feed him while he drove us somewhere fun, and everywhere was fun back then. Maybe we were just riding over to Home Depot to pick up a box of nails. Fun city. How I loved feeding him that fresh, hot fried chickeny gusto-on-a-biscuit on our way to buy nails. Oh boy, did I love it. I loved the crumbs on his lips, the slash of mustard on his chin I'd wipe off with my pinkie. "Tell me another story about your life," I'd ask, again and again. All the picayune stuff about him set my brain on fire. "You tell *me* a story, sugah," he'd say. I swear to God. *Sugah.* I loved feeling womanish, but I loved feeling like pudding even more.

❋   ❋   ❋

IN A FEW years we'd fattened up a bit. We were middle-aged and our metabolisms had slowed, and I guess we were eating more than we danced. What we couldn't resist were the desserts I made, night after night, the *pièce de résistance* after every dinner. Pies and cakes, pies and cakes. If I merely baked cookies, well, that was slumming.

He wanted to lose weight and I did, too. Just a little for me, more for him. He wanted to give up butter and everything that was white: wheat products, sugar, all dairy. For my birthday that year he gave me a cookbook: *The Healthy Kitchen*, by Andrew Weil, MD, and Rosie Daley, Oprah's personal chef. Of course I agreed to help. Mea culpa! I had fattened us up to begin with, so encouraged by a man who swooned over every forkful I cooked that I hadn't paid attention to my culinary terrorism. As previously confessed, I was inclined to fry the hell out of everything. God! The best livers and onion you ever ate in your life! I made this sugar-and-butter loaded decadence called Katherine Hepburn Brownies, not Southern at all, except that I added more of everything—and that's a Southern cook's tendency. We ate dessert every night we were together, and if I left him with a pan of brownies, he polished them off in half a day. He was a dessert-aholic, he said. No control when it came to *sugah*. We agreed that we'd gotten fat, but we'd been so happy! Maybe we were happy enough to go on a diet and be okay.

On our diet, many good things happened: We stopped having second and third helpings; I learned to cook with olive oil. I eliminated salting things altogether (you can use lemon instead of salt). We switched to sweet potatoes. We stopped eating beef—he'd read too many disturbing articles about beef processing. No butter. No milk. No bread. We ate soy ice cream if we wanted something sweet. Or tapioca 'til we choka'd. We used Splenda. Never enda. I think the food I missed most was normal wheat-based pasta. The substitute pasta made with rice and soy was always gummy and tasted gray.

Pounds melted off us like tallow on candles. People noticed. Somebody in my neighborhood asked a good friend of mine if I was sick, maybe doing chemo. *He* said that he'd never felt better in his life, that his digestion had improved and he had more energy. Miraculously, his allergies seemed to have vanished, too. I was dragging, and, after about four months, went on line and discovered that I was three pounds *underweight* for my height. I started adding a dessert to my own diet now and again, but he was so pleased with his newly trim and invigorated self that he wasn't about to budge from a successful regimen.

Years later he would still not eat one of my desserts. He seemed to pride himself on the stoicism of refusal. If we gave a party, he sat smiling like the vegan cat who'd refused to eat the canary while guests lapped up my homemade chocolate pound cake with its "sad streak" of fudgy innards or Coronation Butterscotch Pie, desserts that I associated with our early romance, enticements that he had celebrated and I believed had helped me to bag his affection. Did his rejection of these treats, long after he'd reached his weight-loss goal, beget his dismissal of fun as well? Gradually the playful sparkle in his eyes dulled. He had a few professional disappointments and setbacks (don't we all?), and I couldn't help thinking that a big old slice of coconut cream pie would have cheered him right out of his doldrums in a way the styrofoam crunch of rice cakes did not. Certainly I cajoled and tempted him toward the happy foods of our past—offered in moderation. But he said no, as if to drugs. It was going to be all or nothing, and he chose nothing—with ironclad determination. You don't try to change a sixty-year-old man unless you have experience and past success in moving mountains.

✳ ✳ ✳

AFTER WE PARTED, it was a low time for us both. He learned to cook a little and mostly lived off beans. I rented a sunny studio apartment in Chapel Hill, the first space I had ever rented solo. I'd leased a little cottage when I left my marriage, decades ago, but I had children living with me then.

This tree house, as I call it, in the heart of old Chapel Hill is my first ever home alone. It's one large room over a tree-shaded three-car garage. It's only got half a kitchen—a teensy fridge, a two-burner stove top, a toaster oven, a microwave, a couple of drawers and shelves, a Barbie-size dishwasher—but the west windows overlook a glorious rose garden.

✳ ✳ ✳

ON MOVE-IN DAY, the chief carpenter/contractor commandeers the apartment, tending to some last repairs. She's a sturdy, good-looking, young woman wearing jeans and a tool belt. Her employees are both older men. I note her no-nonsense commands of them, the absence of small talk, her omission of the words *thank you* and *please*. "Go down to the truck," she says to one of them. "Find the bag with screws. If it's not there, go back to Home Depot."

"I'm actually going to Home Depot after the furniture's delivered," I tell her. "Want me to pick up anything for you?"

She sort of snickers. Like, why send a fool shopping when there are men around who will do it and actually know what to buy?

"Where are you going to put the sofa when it comes?" she asks.

"I was thinking maybe . . ."

"It should go here," she says, pointing to the space currently occupied by the table and chairs. "That's the only place it will fit."

"You think so?"

"I do. Guys, move this table and the chairs to the wall over there." They do so immediately.

"Thank you so much," I say as the men skulk off.

"Yep," she says looking the place over. "We had to change the shelf sizes over the stove. The shelves stuck out over the back burner. The narrower shelves work better. You like to cook?"

"I do."

"Well, be careful. Don't burn the place up the first week you're here."

After the furniture arrives and the boss lady contractor arranges it to suit herself, I leave to run errands. It's almost 2 p.m., and I'm suddenly monumentally hungry. Down down down the long Franklin Street hill that runs perpendicular to Estes Drive I roll. Where to get a bite and refuel before shopping? And then, at the bottom of the hill, I spy the sign *Sunrise Biscuits* and I know without a second's hesitation that I'll stop there.

I haven't eaten at Sunrise Biscuits in probably fifteen years. I didn't know it still existed. My man and I, on our diets, had years ago nixed Sunrise from our list of eateries, not only because of the biscuit factor but the fried chicken breast at the heart of its delicious sandwiches.

The bag the server hands me is warm and aromatic. I've ordered our old favorite: chicken biscuit with pickles, mayo, mustard. They load the pickles on—tart coins of perfectly sour green dills. The biscuits are still big and fluffy, scratch-made, golden and crunchy on top. I sneak enough of a nibble to discover that they've not changed the recipe. I can't drive to the nearby park fast enough, where underneath a spindly canopy of wintry limbs, I peel back the paper wrapper, behold, inhale, chomp down. I admire the sunlight sparkling on an oozing pearl of mayo; I turn the sandwich and study its crusty beauty from all angles. There are tears in my eyes as I chew, abandoning myself once again to the sensation of gusto. My lungs feel amplified, breathing the biscuity air. My insides feel petted. I am opening my mouth wider than I have opened it in years to accommodate such behemoth consolation. The chicken tastes as tender as a cloud. Ah, appetite! Let her rip.

MARIANNE GINGHER is the author of the novel *Bobby Rex's Greatest Hit* (which was made into an NBC movie), many short stories, and two memoirs including *Adventures in Pen Land,* about the writing life. Her most recent book, for which she served as editor, is *Amazing Place.* She is also the editor of Eno Publishers' *27 Views of Greensboro.* Co-founder of Jabberbox Puppet Theater, a Greensboro-based venue for puppetry arts, she is currently professor of English and comparative literature at the University of North Carolina at Chapel Hill.

Pollo a la Brasa Keeps Turning in North Carolina

※ PAUL CUADROS ※

IT WAS 1974 and I was on a cold and crowded train with my family traveling from Puno to Cuzco in Perú to discover my roots and to see the country my father so loved and missed. My father was originally from Arequipa, the "white city" to the south. My mother was from the seaside city of Trujillo in the north. They had met in Lima at a carnival dance and fallen in love and married. They had two sons before 1960 when my father emigrated to the United States seeking a better life. I was ten when my father wanted me to know his, our, country. We flew to Lima and from there to Arequipa and then took a train to Cuzco to see Machu Picchu. Our train ran over a pack of mules a farmer was transporting and had to stop for the night at a small village called Sicuani. I remember Sicuani to this day because of two memorable things that happened. The first, my mother's purse was stolen along with our traveler's checks; and the second, a small restaurant in town where we ate while we waited for our train to be repaired.

The tiny restaurant with four tables was the kind of place you can still find in remote rural areas of Latin America. It was essentially a room in someone's house where they had a soda machine and cooked in their kitchen. The specialty was *pollo a la brasa,* or grilled chicken. My brothers and cousin Willie and I ordered the chicken. It was incredible. The most succulent juicy barbecued chicken I had ever eaten. The skin was darkened, crispy, delicate and would dissolve in your mouth before you were done chewing. It was infused with the pungent aroma of cumin so often found in Peruvian food that complimented the chicken perfectly. The flavor had penetrated deep inside the meat of the chicken as well. When I looked down at my plastic plate there was a ring of juice from the chicken circling it.

As much as I loved that chicken, my cousin Willie was in heaven. My father had brought my cousin, his sister's son, on the trip. Willie had no father and my dad was helping to raise him. He was my third brother but different in disposition than myself and my other two brothers. Willie was the exact opposite of my older brother, Al, even though they were close in age, seventeen. He was brash, showy, with long black hair parted in the middle as was the style in the 1970s. He made friends easily and wooed girls with confidence. Later, he would drop out of college to buy a black and gold T-top Trans Am, complete with the firebird on the hood.

Willie devoured his chicken in a flash, washing it down with an orange Fanta. Then he ordered another chicken and another bottle of Fanta. He had a bit of trouble with the third chicken but the Fanta helped, I think. The *dueña*, or owner, approached our table cautiously for the fourth time to see if we were done, but Willie looked at his plate and thought, no, I need another *pollo*. So he ordered another one. And a Fanta. The *dueña's* eyes widened and she turned and walked away slowly. The fourth seemed easier than number three for some reason, and Willie finished it off with no problem. I was stunned. It was getting late and my dad let us know that the train was fixed and about to leave. We left the restaurant with *la dueña* looking at my cousin and telling my dad in Spanish, *"que tremendo!"*

Somewhere in the mountains that night with the train rumbling and careening back and forth those four chickens took on a renewed life of their own inside Willie. Or maybe it was the Fantas sloshing around inside him, the orange fizz bubbling up. But he didn't keep them down for long.

But I can't really blame Willie and his infatuation with *pollo a la brasa*. Once you've tried Peruvian chicken, it's hard not to think about it. If you go to Lima or any city in Perú you will find streets lined with *pollerias*, with whole chickens spinning slowly on a spit as wood coals burn underneath in a specially designed roaster. Men with thick arms stand over cutting boards splitting cooked birds into quarters and halves as fast as they can with two smashing cuts. For decades, a North Carolinian had to drive to Northern Virginia or Maryland to get *pollo a la brasa*. Which is why when Mami Nora's opened up in Durham about ten years ago it was a revelation for me.

Just before Davidson Avenue ends sits the original Mami Nora's where she once prepared tax returns for the Latino community and did *pollo a la brasa* on the side. Nora Palma was born in El Salvador and lived in Maryland before moving to Durham to start her business. It was her son, Ranbir Bakhshi, who grew up in Maryland on *pollo a la brasa*, who had the idea of opening a *polleria* in Durham. He went to culinary school and explored the streets of Lima with his Peruvian stepdad searching for the best recipe for rotisserie chicken. The family pooled its resources and opened Mami Nora's. A fire set the family back at first but they recovered and reopened. Mami Nora herself has since retired from the business and her children have taken it over and pushed it beyond the single family restaurant with big visions of expanding the business.

In 2015, with Ranbir and his sister Ruby in command of the business, they changed the concept and renamed the restaurant Alpaca's Peruvian Charcoal Chicken. Alpaca's is not the old Mami Nora's. It embraces the new trend in fast casual dining that has made other concept restaurants like Chipotle expand and grow across the country. They have since opened three other restaurants, one in Cary, Raleigh, and Sanford. How can you do a unique cuisine from another country and compete in the fast casual dining experience? Alpaca's seems to have found the right mix but it hasn't been easy.

"It was hard at the beginning because you had to educate people about the food," says Ruby. She is tall, thin, with café brown eyes and delicate hands. She is tired when she sits down across from me. The restaurant business is a tough business. With no *pollerias* in North Carolina when they opened, it was difficult to convince people to try their chicken. The flavors are so different from other barbecues. "Once people try it for the first time, they embrace it. That's been one of the best parts about this," she says.

Ruby says they have been true to the flavors of Perú and the style of cooking rotisserie chicken including even importing the charcoal ovens from Lima. Their rotisserie ovens are 100 percent charcoal, she says. While my mother is an excellent cook and has prepared traditional Peruvian dishes like *ceviche, aji de gallina, chupe de camarones*, and *lomo saltado*, finding the right ingredients is a challenge to get the proper flavors. So there is always an inferior quality because ingredients, like *huacatay* (a black mint herb), have to be substituted to make up for what can't be found in American grocery stores. Ruby says she and her brother have worked tirelessly to present as authentic an experience as possible.

Alpaca's offers more than just their wonderful juicy chicken. They have added other Peruvian staples like *lomo saltado*, a beef stir-fry with vegetables served over French fries. At first, customers didn't understand why the stir-fry was served over fries. They experimented with serving them on the side but it wasn't traditional Peruvian *lomo saltado* and went back to the original presentation. This was the right choice as the juice from the tenderloin and other ingredients soak into the potatoes to blend it all together. And Alpaca's also serves *arroz chaufa*, or stir-fried rice Peruvian style, in the tradition of what is called *chifa*. Peruvian cuisine is heavily influenced by the Chinese and Japanese migration to the country. Its cuisine is now considered some of the best in the world because of the mixing of influences and Latin American ingredients. It remains a question as to whether anyone can take a complex cuisine like Peruvian cuisine and pull from it dishes that can be converted into fast casual dining successfully, but Alpaca's has a good concept and is growing. Americans do love barbequed food.

"In Perú, the culinary scene is so diverse," Ruby says perking up. "For a lot of people it's strange to see this Asian influence, but it has impacted a lot of Peruvian food."

Ruby and her brother don't have immediate plans to expand to a fifth restaurant. It seems like they are taking a breather after a flurry of expansion and hard work. Ruby says she is inspired by the hard work, courage, and fortitude of her mother. "My brother and I are on the same page keeping up with new improvements for the restaurant and our knowledge," she says. The Alpaca's in Sanford is toying with drive-thru for instance. "We're doing our best." I ask if they'll ever consider serving *anticuchos*, beef hearts marinated with red peppers and grilled shish-kabob style. "Maybe, as a special," she says undaunted.

For now, they'll keep turning chickens and getting customers, like my cousin Willie, to come back for more. Willie still remembers that chicken fondly despite the mishap and laughs at himself. He blames the Fantas.

PAUL CUADROS is an award-winning investigative journalist and associate professor at the School of Media and Journalism at the University of North Carolina at Chapel Hill. His work has appeared in many publications, including the *New York Times*, *Time* magazine, and *People*. He is the author of *A Home on the Field: How One Championship Soccer Team Inspires Hope for the Revival of Small Town America*, selected as summer reading at five universities and made into a television documentary series, produced by Jennifer Lopez.

Brick Cheese, Boiled Cabbage, and Buttermilk

☀ ELIZABETH S.D. ENGELHARDT ☀

MY MOTHER HAS a sensitive nose. Smells go straight to her head. Particularly troublesome are paint thinners, mothballs, petroleum products, lawn chemicals, glues, turpentine, and dead things. She can be several rooms away, but if you so much as crack open a jar of any of the above, she is knocked out seconds later.

Unfortunately for her nose, she married a chemical engineer. My father filled the basement of their house in Western North Carolina with carefully labeled containers full of industrial-strength preparations. He drove to South Carolina for the "good" pest and weed killers, the ones banned in North Carolina. He had a side business through my childhood repairing cars in the basement and driveway. Broken cars leak, gush, and ooze gasoline, oil, paint, and epoxies. Mom would take to the den at the longest physical distance from his explosions of smells and fumes and quietly sigh.

Nowhere did the battle of smells wage stronger than over food. And no food smelled riper, with more stench, and over a greater area of impact than Dad's Wisconsin-born brick cheese.

This is the story of a table where the people mesh easily but their foods do not. For every romantic tale of breaking bread together at a Carolina table, for every sweet conversion to a new land brought about by trading lovingly prepared, flavorful bites for gifts of new tastes in return, there sits one food that proves a bridge too far. In this case, it threatened to shut down the town post office, was the source of a formal grievance filed at the local factory, and segregated an upstairs refrigerator and freezer from a downstairs set, locked in a permanent standoff of close to fifty years running.

Western North Carolina, and indeed all of Appalachia, is experiencing a food renaissance. People search for heritage foods; compose loving photo-essays of its tables; produce glossy cookbooks; and flock to pop-up dinners celebrating Appalachian foodways simple and complex.[1] Ripe, rich, smelly, and stinky foods can be found throughout the newly celebrated mountain food traditions. Ask people to name an Appalachian food and they may well come up with the smelliest of them all: ramps. Legendary wild onions, ramps ooze through your skin, hang in a house, and coat a valley. They cause nonbelievers to beg they not be disturbed, much less eaten. Devotees dig them with special hoes, follow old paths to patches, and harness social media to spread news of early sightings each spring.

My mother's family was not enthusiastic about ramps, only occasionally bringing some home to freezers after trips to community festivals. Still, the family had its own smelly food traditions. The cloying flatness of my grandmother's boiled cabbage hit my senses as soon as I reached the porch on the way into her kitchen on winter days. It stayed in my nose no matter how much rich macaroni and cheese or fresh angel food cake my eight-year-old self tried discreetly to sniff while eating. Pickled beans, beets, carrots, and onions offered their own twitch to the nose, sometimes accompanied by the boss of them all: kraut. I have an uncle who still swears by his dose of apple cider vinegar every day,

---

1. The Appalachian Food Summit, recipient of the 2015 John Egerton Award from the Southern Foodways Alliance, held its third regional symposium in Fall 2016 at Berea, Kentucky. Among Appalachian cities, Asheville leads in pop-up dinners, such as those by the Blind Pig group. In the *Washington Post,* Jane Black declared, "The Next Big Thing in American Regional Cooking: Humble Appalachia," 29 March 2016, https://www.washingtonpost.com/lifestyle/food/the-next-big-thing-in-american-regional-cooking-humble-appalachia/2016/03/28/77da176a-f06d-11e5-89c3-a647fcce95e0_story.html. Cookbooks include Sean Brock's *Heritage* (Artisan, 2014) and Ronni Lundy's *Victuals: An Appalachian Journey with Recipes* (Clarkson Potter, 2016). For more on this new interest, see my own "Appalachian Chicken and Waffles: Countering Southern Food Fetishism," *Southern Cultures* 21.1 (Spring 2015), 73–83.

the uncorking of which can overpower a room. Even the longstanding family prescription to settle a troublesome belly, fresh buttermilk, wafts tendrils of sharpness into the air and causes those spots on either side of your throat to catch tightly as it slides down to coat your insides against further twinges. Today, people exchange leads for where to find the best, strongest, richest buttermilk for sale like they are stock tips—guarded, rarely shared, and robustly valued.

In the 1970s, though, recipes in our house were more likely from *Southern Living* than old mountain knowledge; bridge party food reigned as the pinnacle of food preparation; and cheese in Western North Carolina was rarely adventuresome. It was American, and it was orange. For special treats, mild, rubbery "Swiss" or gentle, inoffensive "cheddar" appeared, but this was before even the relative wildness of the Havarti years. Bleu cheese dressing was "blue" and creamy but not fragrant. Hickory Farms might add the tiniest bite to their cheese balls as a holiday special. Occasionally, my mother and friends sprinkled essence of cayenne into the cheese straws but only for rare evening bridge parties, and never too much.

My father loved almost everything about his new mountain home. He arrived in the early 1960s, fresh from college and his time in service. Aided by a love of alpine skiing, he transitioned easily from his flat beginnings in snowy Wisconsin to the higher but shorter winter mountain cultures of the South. Polka became square dancing. Cream of Wheat became grits. Cherry orchards in Door County became apple trees on the Blue Ridge Parkway. But he did not love the South's cheese-like products. His family had owned a dairy in Green Bay, and he yearned for the sharpness, bite, layers, and smell of real cheese. He did the only logical thing: He smuggled it in.

We took a family vacation to Wisconsin every eighteen months (summer one time; Christmas the next). Dad packed the family car, a process that used the entire driveway, maps on graph paper, and an official ranking from each of us about which containers we needed to reach quickly and which we could forego until our final destination. Somehow, despite the family only numbering three, trips always involved me sharing the backseat with luggage, furniture, or antique car parts because the trunk was so full. Many times I rode the thousand miles without putting my feet on the floorboards or tucked into a tiny corner of the seat with large items secured by the other two seatbelts. However full the car was as we started out from Hendersonville, Dad always managed to bring along an empty cooler.

It was an astonishing waste of space—until the trek home made the decision clear. While in Wisconsin, Dad purchased a range of cheddars, beautiful mild ones and tangy sharp ones. He added in soft cheeses, Swiss cheeses with flavor and texture, and cheeses for melting and shredding, enough to last for months to come. And he swore that was all. But deep in the recesses of that cooler, frozen and surrounded by ice and freezer packs (and one notable year, in a container holding dry ice), wrapped in plastic and aluminum foil, and sealed into additional, heavy-duty plastic bags, nestled his prize haul. He carefully changed the ice at every stop, which was extraordinary for a man otherwise devoted to economy and thrift. Each time, we raced back South, taking no detours or side trips along the way.

As the heat rose, my mother began to sniff. She moved around in her seat. And when she could not take anymore, she started to question: "What IS that smell?" "Did you?" and then, *"Bob!"* He would quickly exit the interstate for a surreptitious change of packaging.

It was the brick cheese. You may think bleu cheese has a smell. You may point to Limburger or the Epoisses de Bourgogne that is banned from public transportation in France. If you get a young brick cheese, you will likely declare its flavor positively mild. Even many blocks sold as aged brick cheese today are relatively smooth and inoffensive. Perhaps, too, our collective palates have changed and we are just more familiar and comfortable with the smelly, stinky, and ripe in our cheese choices. Brick cheese is a Wisconsin-specific development, dating to small cheese makers in the late nineteenth century. It is pressed with a brick, possibly contributing to its name. Its distinctive smell comes from aging that allows *bacterium linens* to develop. Kin to those Limburgers and bleu cheeses, brick cheese was an acquired taste even among dairy-centric Wisconsin food cultures.[2] On our family road trips back to North Carolina, brick cheese was a hazardous chemical, treated with care and protocol.

My mother was not the only person brick cheese caused such concern. Once, my grandfather shipped a package of it through the U.S. mail from Wisconsin to North Carolina. Hendersonville's post office had a reputation for not notifying people when packages arrived; much like a Carol Burnett skit, they just could not be bothered. They skipped right past the "swift completion" portion of "neither snow nor rain nor heat nor gloom of night." Yet two days into a summer heat wave, our home phone started ringing: "Mr. Delwiche, we aren't sure what all you've been shipped. Seems like it might have died, though. Seems like you ought to get yourself down here and pick it up. We're talking ASAP, if you wouldn't mind. Otherwise, we might just have to shut down this whole facility."

When rescued from the post office and unpacked from the cooler, brick cheese found its way into Dad's lunchbox to be eaten in the factory cafeteria. Even more of Western North Carolina took a sniff and declared a state of emergency. One staff member bustled down the hall to find proper forms to file a formal complaint, especially offended that a communal toaster oven was used to melt the cheese in its sandwich. Meanwhile, women responsible for the cafeteria, who had not seen the offending melt, frantically closed down lunch service and instituted a massive all-hands-on-deck search to move equipment out from walls, shine lights under, around, and in dark recesses of the facility, determined to find the source of the desperate fumes creeping through the entire factory.[3]

2. For a history of brick cheese, from a maker's perspective, see http://www.widmers cheese.com/the-story-of-wisconsin-brick-cheese/. Our family dairy, Delwiche Farms, specialized in milks and ice creams and never made cheeses, so Dad's taste came from elsewhere.

3. Dad notes here that as soon as he realized the cafeteria workers' worry, he slipped in the side door to tell them quietly what was going on. The formal complaint he never admitted to—given that the brick cheese had left the factory, he did assert confidently there was no ongoing problem.

The cheese, then, was sent back home but banned from upstairs. Exiled, it sat in the downstairs freezer and refrigerator, next to batteries and packages of ramps, near but not touching the year's supply of Georgia pecans, a floor and a series of compromises distant from the upstairs buttermilk, pickles, and vinegars. Dad only dared indulge on nights when Mom was at bridge and I was tucked safely into bed. Occasionally he found a weekend day when Mom was shopping. He calculated his cooking adventures to begin as soon as she pulled out of the driveway. If he felt particularly brave, he would go all out and add sardines to the patty melt, figuring in for a smelly penny, in for an odorous pound. Afterward, he scrubbed the used pan with specially purchased Brillo pads. He opened wide every window and every door, even the creaky sliding door that always went off its rail. He installed an attic fan powerful enough to lift papers from the kitchen table to catch the North Carolina air and release the Wisconsin fumes—to no avail.

One step out of her car, still in the driveway, before she even placed a toe on the walkway, Mom sensed it. Her nose caught the first whiff. Her head prepared to ache. While the rest of North Carolina might not have known what to do with Appalachia's ramps, buttermilk, and boiled cabbage, neither she nor the mountains were ready for the particular Wisconsin bouquet of brick cheese. On those nights, our Carolina table moved outside to the picnic table, and we ate anything but cheese at our own pop-up dinner under the stars.

Native North Carolinian, ELIZABETH S.D. ENGELHARDT is the John Shelton Reed Distinguished Professor of Southern Studies in American Studies at the University of North Carolina at Chapel Hill. She serves on several boards, including the Southern Foodways Alliance. Her most recent books include *Mess of Greens* and *The Republic of Barbecue*. After venturing out of state for several years, she is thrilled to be back, close to her parents (who still live in Hendersonville), as well as the birds, trees, mountains, and sea of her home state.

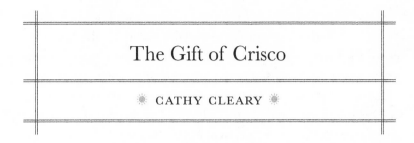

The Gift of Crisco

※ CATHY CLEARY ※

AS A LONG-TERM vegetarian I was puzzled by my husband's interest in meat-eating—pork-eating in particular. Across the dinner table, I would watch Reid close his eyes and swoon as he chewed pieces of sausage. I didn't understand, but I wanted to.

Reid loves to eat, and I love to cook for him. I love to feed everyone, but he is my favorite person to think about while I'm exploring flavor combinations. I enjoy figuring out what he likes to eat and why. Yet, his enthusiasm for pork remained a mystery.

I suspected his Eastern North Carolina upbringing was responsible for his pork passion. I grew up in North Carolina too; but my hometown of Chapel Hill is not exactly the heart of traditional Southern cooking. Oh sure, my family participated in neighborhood pig pickin's. But I remember the community ritual of those events more than the finished product. I was a bit of a rebel, having proclaimed my vegetarianism at a young age, probably before I'd even tasted that slow-cooked barbecue.

The more I reflected on my lack of exposure to pork and meat in general, the more I realized how it limited me as a cook. So, I decided to explore meat-eating for myself, and for Reid. Which led me to Crisco the pig.

As the owner of a café at the beginning of the farm-to-table movement, I befriended quite a few local farmers. My farmer friend, Tom, told me one day that he'd won a pig at a greased-pig contest and named him Crisco. Tom then asked if he could take my three-day-old breads and pastries back to his farm to fatten up Crisco. I gladly obliged.

That summer Reid and I went out to Tom's farm and met Crisco. He had a set-up—a good-sized pen with plenty of shady trees and nice dark brown mud, a gorgeous view of the Pisgah Mountain range, pastries and artisan bread for breakfast. Not a bad life.

But one always wants more. Crisco was a master escape artist and had been getting into mischief. Tom grew dozens of varieties of heirloom garlic, and what pig wouldn't enjoy a little heirloom garlic with his artisan bread. Tom had chased Crisco around and watched him eat up garlic meant for market one too many times. As summer turned to fall, the chase was up. It was time for Crisco to become what he was always destined to be—sausage.

Tom asked if he could use my commercial kitchen for the processing. Reid's birthday was coming up, and I'd been wondering what to get him. So, Tom and I struck a deal: He could use my kitchen if he would sell me half of Crisco. Tom liked that idea fine. At the time he was a single guy, and three hundred pounds of pork was more than he needed.

Hog-killing time requires just the right set of circumstances. It's best done on a cold and dry day, and in this case it needed to happen on a weekend so that everyone involved in the process would be available. But the weather was not cooperating. So Tom sent me a side view picture of Crisco, and that is what I gave to Reid for his birthday.

The side view meant that you could only see half the pig, which seemed appropriate since Reid's present was just half of Crisco. I'm not exactly sure what reaction I expected, but his delight and excitement were unparalleled in our gift-giving history. He carried Crisco's picture around in his shirt pocket and anytime there was a lull in conversation Reid would pull out the picture and say, "Look at what my wonderful wife gave me for my birthday!"

Most folks thought I had given him a pet, and wondered where we could keep such a large animal in our postage-stamp-sized yard. Reid quickly explained that Crisco would not be on the hoof much longer.

Then he got one of two reactions: wide-eyed, mouth-watering envy or nose-wrinkled disgust. He seemed oblivious that anyone might be offended. His joy could not be contained.

Finally, one sunny, cold Saturday, Carvin' Arvin, the traveling butcher, did the deed. Arvin arrived at Tom's farm with his tools, and, using kindness and reverence, he dispatched Crisco. Reid was there as Arvin deftly cut out the hams, ribs, sidemeat, and loins. Much of the meat was set aside for sausage-making, which I would oversee in the cafe kitchen.

We invited several of Reid's most enthusiastic pork-loving friends. With sausage-making books on hand, and a borrowed grinding attachment for my powerful sixty-quart Hobart mixer, we were ready for the huge coolers full of Crisco as soon as they arrived. Pounds and pounds of lean pork and fat were ground together, seasoned, and stuffed into casings. Someone brought beer, and with each batch of sausage, we fried up tastings to make sure the seasoning was right. Meanwhile we salted hams and rubbed sidemeat with spices for future curing and smoking. Admittedly, I had some trepidation about the whole process, given my herbivore history, but I was surprised by how much it felt like a party.

That evening, covered in sausage grease and a beer in hand, I decided it was time. After seventeen years as a vegetarian, I needed a taste of Crisco. I reasoned that Crisco had lived a good life, eating well, lounging, and getting into mischief here and there. Not only that, but a party was being thrown in his honor. It seemed I should honor him by joining the tasting party.

I vividly remember that bite of sausage. The flavors of garlic, parsley, and chilies melded with warm, juicy, tender meat. The seasoning was perfect. I closed my eyes and swooned.

CATHY CLEARY is founder and former co-owner of West End Bakery and Cafe in West Asheville. She lives and works with food and gardens in Asheville. As co-founder of the nonprofit FEAST, she believes that everyone deserves to eat wholesome food every day. She published the *West End Bakery and Cafe Cookbook* in 2014 and is at work on another cookbook, celebrating regional seasonal produce, which will be published by Eno Publishers.

Let's Cook, EXCLAMATION POINT

☀ MICHAEL PARKER ☀

THAT THERE MIGHT not have actually been an exclamation point at the end of the cooking column my mother wrote for my father's weekly newspaper in the Seventies is only further proof of the merciless irony shared by me and my four siblings. Everything—school, politics, our choir director's too-small Hang Ten lime green pantsuit, our wacky fundamentalist neighbor who came over to our house on rainy days and sang *Nearer My God to Thee* in a vibratoed lisp—was fodder for our trash-talking. Every other word out of our mouths was couched in quotation marks, italicized by smart-assedness. The great gulf between the way the world might have seemed to those outside the immediate family and the way we pitched it makes such slight matters of punctuation irrelevant, for to our minds the name of the column was always announced with exaggerated exuberance. LET'S COOK!

We had other names for it. Because a high percentage of the recipes called for a package of dried powder, we called it LET'S COOK WITH LIPTON'S ONION SOUP! In that era of polyester and Fresca, much of what was called salad contained marshmallows or carrot slivers quivering in translucent cubes of Jell-O, which led us to call the column LET'S COOK SOME SALAD WITHOUT ANY LETTUCE IN IT! My mother's cooking column was the subject of much scrutiny because my mother, as she would herself admit, was not really all that into cooking. She was too busy. She worked as dean of students for a community college and she ran the evening program and traveled around our huge county—bigger in square mileage than the state of Rhode Island—recruiting recent high school grads. Often her workday began at 8 a.m. and ended past 9 p.m. There wasn't much time to spend planning elaborate meals for her brood, none of whom were terribly discriminating. As long as there was a gallon of milk on the table to wash down the casserole and canned Le Sueur peas, we were happy. We ate a lot of baked spaghetti (my favorite part of which remains the crusty edges, scraped from the perimeter of Pyrex) and we ate a lot of Hamburger Helper. I grew up loving Hamburger Helper. I especially loved the title—the notion that the scalloped potatoes were just there to lend a helping hand to the hamburger led my brothers and sisters and me to break into an impromptu chorus of "You've Got a Friend" every time the dish appeared on the dinner table, which was every other night.

Because my parents came of age in the Depression in large families—my mother is the last of seven, my father the last of eight—food was not something they were inclined to be ironic about. On the rare occasions when my father cooked, his two specialties were something he called Scrambled Hamburger, which was ground beef browned and plated and presented to us as if it were *foie gras* (apparently his hamburger did not need any help), and Welsh Rarebit, which I can only assume that my father, a working-class boy from Tarboro, North Carolina, picked up while overseas during World War II. Even though we tried to attack the latter dish with our characteristic irony, calling it English Rabbit, its simplicity—as I remember, a puddle of melted cheese over toast—put it in the same category as Flaubert's limited heroine Félicité, in "A Simple Heart," about whom the literary critic Jonathon Culler, in answer to those who read the author's treatment of her as cruelly ironic, argued that there was nothing there for irony to deflate.

My mother agreed to write her cooking column not because she was interested in cooking but because my father's newspaper did not have a cooking column. Nor did the rival paper, the Republican one, across town. A cooking column was needed, my mother was a woman, women wrote cooking columns.

Running a small town newspaper in the 1970s was a family affair. My brothers and sisters and I spent our Wednesday afternoons shuffling the sections together and wrapping up the papers and stuffing them into heavy canvas bags to ferry to the post office. My father was nominally the editor and publisher, but he did everything from write columns and photograph wrecks and freakishly giant gourds to help lay the paper out and stamp address labels. His schedule was every bit as hectic as my mother's, and he often came home for supper only long enough to shout down Jesse Helms, who had a gig at as a television commentator on a station out of Raleigh, scarf down his Hamburger Helper, and head back to the office.

My mother was not hopeless in the kitchen. Every Sunday after church we sat down to a memorable pot roast, stewed with carrots and potatoes. After the five of us left home, it seemed she grew more inventive: I remember a stir-fry period, replete with well-oiled wok, a rarity in Eastern North Carolina in the Eighties. But her passions were, and still are, liberal politics and Carolina basketball, not necessarily in that order, and I suspect that feeding five ironic children was enough of a burden that flavor, much less presentation or variety, was not even close to being a priority. Though some prowess in the kitchen might seem a prerequisite for a cooking column, my father's paper was not, as I mentioned, governed by specialization. (The sportswriter was a community theater type, bearded and black-turtle-necked, beatnik-ish; his write-ups of Friday night football reflected more his passion for outdoor "symphonic dramas" than what happened on the field.) Every week my mother sifted through cookbooks and collected things that she thought might appeal to the citizens of Clinton, North Carolina. Sometimes she wrote a few words of introduction, but she kept her comments to a minimum. She approached the task with the alacrity and efficiency that had led her to go back to school for a counseling certificate at night while three of her children were still at home. I have no memory of whether she ever actually cooked anything she featured in her column, but I suspect that if she did, she followed the recipe faithfully, for a recipe is finally a plan. My mother knew that, in order to survive, a plan must be followed, and she made and implemented her plans the way my father scrambled hamburger, attaching to each task an exclamation point free of irony.

MICHAEL PARKER is the author of six novels and two collections of short fiction. His nonfiction has appeared in the *New York Times*, the *Washington Post*, *The Oxford American*, *Men's Journal*, *Our State*, and *Runner's World*. He is the recipient of a Pushcart Prize, two O. Henry awards, a National Endowment for the Arts fellowship, and the North Carolina Award for Literature. He teaches literature and creative writing at the University of North Carolina at Greensboro.

TRADITIONS

The Family Reunion

※ NANCIE McDERMOTT ※

I REMEMBER THE family reunions of my childhood with pleasure and gratitude, and with remarkable clarity, given how many details I have forgotten from a decade or two ago. Surely this is because these long-ago celebrations centered around my favorite subject, food. Once a year, on the second Sunday in June, my maternal grandmother joined her brothers and sisters and their descendants for a covered dish meal of epic proportions. She was one of twelve brothers and sisters, born to Cad Wallander and Mary Elizabeth Lloyd at the end of the nineteenth century, most of whom spent their lives within a hundred miles of their homeplace in Hillsborough, North Carolina.

The Lloyd family had been gathering for big summertime family reunions for years before I came along. Originally, hosting duties rotated among the homes of the brothers and sisters—many of them dairy farmers in Orange County. I treasure a large black and white photograph of an early reunion on the lawn in front of my grandparents' big white farmhouse. A professional photographer was called in, with the kind of camera that panned slowly left to right, capturing a CinemaScopic portrait of the wide wonderful world of grandparents, uncles, aunties, and cousins. On the far left is my father with his big glasses and a bigger grin. He stands beside my mother, looking pretty with curly hair and a shirtwaist dress, and holding two-year-old me. My slightly older sister beams from her spot on the grass in the front row of cousins, those old enough to escape parental oversight and sit, squirming and giggling, at the feet of their seated elders.

My memories commence a few years later, after the reunion out-grew the home venues. The new location was Schley Grange, a large, red-brick community center in the northeastern corner of Orange County, some fifteen miles from my grandparents' farm. Grange halls date back to the 1870s and have long served as gathering places for political and social events in agricultural communities around the country, especially in the South. Schley Grange made an ideal venue for the family reunion, with its great high-ceilinged, window-lined hall, enormous professional kitchen, numerous bathrooms, profusion of shade trees surrounding it, and a softball diamond for afternoon diversions.

Renting the grange included access to stacks of long tables and an abundance of folding chairs. Numerous screen-covered windows lined the main room, mostly covered by long cloth shades to mute the midday sun, but open enough to invite passing breezes.

The soundtrack for the day remains clear in my mind. First comes a sharp and steady percussion, the screen door slamming as gaggles of cousins scoot in and out of the cool, cavernous entrance hall. Stern but futile commands to "Quit Slamming That Door" fade into the more musical notes from the kitchen: a soprano hum of aunts and great-aunts, my grandmother and my mother, bustling about. Ice cubes clink and then tumble into large metal dispensers of sweet tea. The women stack plates, set out serving utensils, and wrap forks and spoons in paper napkins, sharing news, dividing up chores, and deciding how soon to call everyone inside for the blessing.

When my mother had deposited her dishes in the great room and joined her sisters in the kitchen, I quietly entered the hall on my re-connaissance mission. Knowing what-foods-were-placed-where not only filled me with eager joy, but enabled me to orchestrate my final approach to the long container-filled rows of culinary delights. Since my family tends toward tardiness, the serving tables in the great hall were already crowded with food, squeezed onto almost every inch of tablecloth. Platters, plates, bowls, and casserole dishes had been set in place by countless early-arriving and on-time aunts, great-aunts, and older cousins. For a few sweet minutes, I would have the room all to myself.

Once I had entered undetected, I scouted the cloth-draped tables, lined up end to end in three or four long rows. Beyond the stacks of dinner plates, our feast's cool beginnings lay in colorful, sparkling profusion. Pickles and preserves reigned. My grandmother and her sisters and sisters-in law had pulled mason jars from their pantries, spooning their best handiwork into cut-glass bowls: sweet and dill pickles, sharp chow chow and other tangy relishes, sour cherry preserves, and pickled peaches studded with cloves. My mother's generation of cooks had contributed pickled beets, pimento-stuffed olives, tomato aspic, bridge mix, celery sticks stuffed with pimento cheese, and cucumbers and onions baptized in a quick brine.

Everybody brought deviled eggs made their favorite way: soft or firm filling, smoothed out or piled up, with or without pickle relish stirred in, dusted with paprika or not—with most contributions arranged on dedicated deviled-egg plates. Stacks of sandwiches landed here too, filled with creamy store-bought chicken salad and pimento cheese spread over the softest, least-nutritious slices of store-bought white bread money could buy. Tomatoes weren't ripe until July, so tomato sandwiches, that great simple Southern summertime treat, were absent from our June reunion bounty.

Next up were the hearty dishes, with fried chicken in greatest abundance. I paid little attention here, since there was plenty to choose from and I knew every single piece of fried chicken would be gloriously good. Baked ham was well represented, with towering stacks of thick, pink slices arranged on platters. Back then, commercially baked, spiral-cut hams were but a dream in a food entrepreneur's eye, and the line would not have paused graciously while one family member after another carved off a good piece. I noted which country ham biscuits looked fluffiest and seemed most generously supplied with crisp, salty ham, while also scouting for cube steak in gravy and stew beef with rice. I ignored the occasional plates of salmon patties and meatloaf, as these were in regular rotation on our supper table at home.

My goal was to spot my favorite reunion contribution: Aunt Julia's chicken pie. My Great-Aunt Julia Lloyd, married to my grandmother's beloved little brother Andrew, was justifiably famous for her chicken pie. Many relatives arrived at the reunion with designs on this annual treat, so advance knowledge of its location was key to my scoring a serving.

Aunt Julia's chicken pie filled an enormous pan, lined with and covered by a generous swath of perfect golden brown pastry, flaky and rich, like an enormous double-crust fruit pie. The savory filling was simple yet divine: chunks of chicken, enrobed in white sauce, seasoned with salt and pepper. That was it. No herbs, no spices, neither peas nor carrots, and no secret sauce. This pie was made from chicken, the local, hormone-free, organic, and free-range variety that she had surely raised from an egg in her own henhouse. Milk and butter in the white sauce and pie crust came from the cows on her family's dairy farm. I knew it shared a name with the individually frozen chicken pot pies in diminutive tinfoil pie pans, which were often my quick lunch or supper at home. But beyond the name and form, these two chicken pies were worlds apart, and Aunt Julia's version was always the first dish to disappear from the family reunion tables.

Next came the cherished category of *threes*, the vegetables, casseroles, Jell-O–based creations, and what passed for salads in my food universe. I call them threes, because they are the catchall of options one might find at a meat-'n'-three, the traditional Southern dining establishment offering guests a choice of one of several meats (think meatloaf, chicken and dumplings, smothered pork chops, and the like) and three of a dozen or so items within the broad category I have outlined, charmingly known throughout the South to this day as *vegetables*.

These Southern so-called vegetables included personal favorites galore: macaroni and cheese—of the baked, custardy kind, not the creamy cheesy modern kind—mashed potatoes, candied yams, squash casserole, coleslaw, potato salad, applesauce, and fried apples. Actual vegetable dishes awaited serving spoons, too: creamed corn, green beans with new potatoes, field peas with snaps, butter beans, succotash, stewed tomatoes, and black-eyed peas. No need to stake these out, as there was always plenty, even for seconds. The young moms contributed carrot-raisin salad, cottage cheese with pineapple, and baked beans. Yet to come were Seventies' specialties: three-bean salad, seven-layer salad, green bean casserole, pasta salad, broccoli casserole, and tomato pie.

Next to the vegetables stood the jiggling rainbow-colored section of what are still referred to as congealed salads—the least appetizing food category name I have ever encountered. Not the colorful, sweet, cool creations themselves, which I liked, but the unappetizing nature of the word *congealed*. My mother's contribution to this division was Golden Glow Salad, a square pan of orange Jell-O, enhanced with grated carrots, crushed pineapple, and chopped pecans. I loved it and still do, but why eat anything from our house, when adventure and variety called out to me from every platter and bowl?

By the time I had cased this much of the joint, serving time was imminent, and I had to focus on the grand finale: desserts. First I got eyes on my grandmother's fresh coconut cake, a beautiful multi-layered creation with a translucent and delicate glaze of grated coconut enrobing a handsome tower of thin yellow cake layers. The cake was familiar to me, but not so common that I would let an opportunity to partake of it pass me by. She made it twice yearly, at Christmas and for the family reunion, and December was too long to wait. Next on my list was Aunt Thelma's caramel cake, a rare treat that like my grandmother's contribution was sure to disappear before the first car headed for home. Pound cakes abounded, iced and plain, round and baked in loaves. Chocolate layer cakes revealed tiny, dense layers of yellow cake, encased in dark chocolate icing, smooth and thin but so rich that it broke off in big bite-sized shards as the cake was cut.

Next came flights of pies, from basic egg custard and chess pies to coconut custard pies, syrup pies, and deeply chocolate pies crowned with brown-tipped weeping meringue. I hunted for squares of luscious fudge, studded with black walnuts or pecans. The younger generation of cooks brought their A-game as well, including pecan pies, strawberry pies, applesauce spice cakes with creamy vanilla icing, frosted cupcakes, and peach cobbler, made with canned peaches and a sweet biscuit topping. One of my aunts brought her moist banana bread made with wheat germ and bran cereal, and the other shared her magnificent German chocolate cake, another certain-to-disappear creation.

A few years hence, the dessert table would include fewer old-school items and more mid-century modern treats, from carrot cake and hummingbird cake, to tunnel-of-fudge cake, and various sweet treats baked in a Bundt pan. Blackberries, like tomatoes, were absent from the spread due to the early-June date of our reunion. Within a month or so, my cousins and I would be back out near Schley Grange with our grandmother, tumbling out of her enormous white Ford Galaxie, parked on the shoulder of the two-lane country road. Braving bugs, thorns, and the fierce July sunshine, we would pull ripe, juicy blackberries from the wild canes flourishing on its banks and in its ditches. Tough work, but my grandmother's blackberry rolls, jams, preserves, and pies were worth every scratch, itch, and sunburn.

My reverie and plotting session ended on the first call to come eat. It emanated from the grange's kitchen and flowed through the screen door, to be picked up and amplified by the menfolk gathered under the shade trees. It took what seemed like an hour for everyone to assemble in the big, cool room, now with lights on and abuzz with conversation.

Blessing time! One of the most senior men stood to say grace, intoning mournfully and taking longer than I liked. But we had much to be thankful for, and it ended, and the lines took shape and began to inch along. I scooted here and there to acquire my most treasured menu items, and then headed for the kids' tables to enjoy my feast.

After dinner (which this was, since it was a huge family meal at midday rather than an evening supper), people dispersed—the women to clean up and visit, the men to smoke, converse, snooze in chairs, and eventually start up a softball game over on the red clay field. I watched a little, played with my cousins, napped, or curled up with my book, and listened out for the call to come get some ice cream, hand-cranked in old-time freezers by the uncles and male cousins.

Finally we said goodbyes and piled into the car, breaking up our two-hour drive home with a long stop at my grandparents' farm. Our first cousins were there too, and we played, napped, made up stories, explored the henhouse, named the calves, and gathered at sunset for a meal of cold fried chicken, deviled eggs, potato salad, pickles, macaroni and cheese, sandwiches, and ham biscuits, along with cucumbers from the garden.

Nowadays we Lloyd family descendants still gather for a reunion the second Sunday in June. We meet at a smaller, handier grange hall, just a few miles outside Chapel Hill near my grandparents' church, in whose cemetery a number of the elders have been laid to rest. On the short drive from home, we pass right by the dairy farm where my grandmother cracked and grated coconuts, patted out biscuit dough, fried chickens, and deviled eggs. I love looking up the long driveway to the front porch and big shade trees, toward the stretch of lawn where lots and lots of Lloyds lined up long ago for that big, black and white photograph.

Nowadays, turnout is in the dozens, rather than the hundreds, and we of the long-ago kids' table are now the elders, remarking in wonder at how adorable the babies are, how much the kids have grown, and how good it is to have made it through another year. We are thankful for the blessing of air conditioning, which incidentally solves forever the problem of the slamming screen door.

The food suits the times: There's fast-food fried chicken, spicy and delicious, with fluffy biscuits on the side. I love it and love being spared the choice between standing over a skillet of hot grease or doing without. We have us a feast, with field peas, butter beans, lima beans and corn, turnip greens, squash casserole, baked beans, potato salad, and coleslaw. Somebody always brings that broccoli salad I love but never get around to making, the one with mayonnaise, red onion, bacon, and pecans. My husband appreciates the sweet and sour meatballs, teriyaki chicken wings, and the potato chips with onion dip. He also enjoys not having to play softball in the heat or take a turn on the ice cream freezer. Desserts rock, with pound cakes, pineapple upside-down cake, applesauce spice cake, punchbowl cake, strawberry shortcake, brownies, cookies, and a fine array of pies including chess, buttermilk, lemon icebox, and pecan.

This year I meant to make my grandmother's fresh coconut cake, but the week got away from me and I didn't get to it. I made a chocolate cake, and chess pie, and deviled eggs served on one of my two dedicated deviled-egg plates. I love that we still have the family reunion, even though it has changed over time. We former screen-door-slamming, lightning-bug-catching, blackberry-picking, comic-book-reading, kids'-table-sitting Lloyd family descendants have changed, too, and it's good to see our younger reinforcements moving along the path. I'm grateful to those who have kept it going all these years, with no help from me. I always look forward to the second Sunday in June, with or without that coconut cake.

Born and raised in Piedmont North Carolina, NANCIE McDERMOTT is a food writer, cookbook author, and cooking teacher. After graduating from the University of North Carolina at Chapel Hill, she spent three years as a Peace Corps volunteer in Thailand, where she fell in love with Asian cooking. Her cookbooks explore home cooking and food traditions in Asian cuisines, as well as in the American South. After years in Thailand, Japan, New York City, and Southern California, she came home to North Carolina and lives with her family in Chapel Hill.

Mountain Cooking

❋ MICHAEL MCFEE ❋

A FEW MONTHS ago, I had lunch at a "destination restaurant" in my native North Carolina mountains, one that says it "tells the story of historic Appalachian cuisine in a picturesque setting." What I ate was tasty enough, though it didn't tell me a story or seem particularly historic. And though I guess such a term is inevitable when a nouvelle eatery has an executive chef, *Appalachian cuisine* sort of stuck in my Blue Ridge craw.

But it did set me to thinking about mountain cooking. I don't mean my Arden mother's, which was mid-twentieth-century-suburban bland: She herself admitted that she didn't much like to cook. I don't even mean my Asheville grandmother's, which was much more authentic and toothsome, particularly at holiday feasts: If there is a heaven, and if—an even bigger conditional—I make it there, I hope the first thing I'm served is a big slice of her divine coconut cake. I mean cooking as it was practiced and enjoyed by common folks way out in the hills, back before food got so fast and drink got so homogenized, and way before upscale establishments arose to tell the story of historic Appalachian cuisine.

My favorite window onto mountain cooking is, in fact, called *Mountain Cooking*, a 1978 book by John Parris, writer and editor for the Asheville *Citizen-Times* for forty-two years. (That newspaper published five fat hardback collections of his columns, with nice flora and fauna line drawings by his wife Dorothy. Those were the journalistic days.) Mom loved his "Roaming the Mountains" triweekly pieces in the paper, folksy stories about Western North Carolina people and places—their work and crafts, their family or community traditions, and especially what they ate and drank, the focus of this collection, which gathers eighty-seven columns and three hundred or so recipes, some informally included in the stories and others arranged in eight categories at the back: *Appetizers; Sandwiches and Soups; Meat, Poultry, and Other Main Dishes; Game; Vegetables, Main Dish Accompaniments, and Salads; Breads, Pies, Cakes, Desserts, Cookies, and Candies; Pickles, Preserves, and Relishes;* and *Beverages.*

Parris celebrates mountaineers like "Aunt Tennie, who was born in 1886 over in the Sugar Fork hills of Macon County," "a right smart woman with a skillet. She isn't a fancy cook. But she can take simple and inexpensive things and make them pleasure the palate." That's a good description of his own writing style, which seems fairly straight-forward but often makes its way to unexpectedly tasty turns of phrase and bursts of flavor. The first piece, "Conjuring Up Old Memories," is typical. It includes a specific dateline, "Laurel Cove," it makes clear the time of year ("when the first icy winds come prowling under the eaves"), and it focuses—in nostalgic but imaginative ways—on "Grandma's cooking" and recollections "of long-remembered aromas drifting from the kitchen and long-remembered tastes that a small boy somehow loses with growing up, forever haunting and elusive." (Yes, Parris has drunk deep at the well of Thomas Wolfe. But his sentences are firmly rooted in all five senses.) The next paragraph elaborates: "They are memories of buckwheat cakes and sorghum molasses and fresh homemade sausage of a peppermint morning and of Grandpa sitting at the big table in the kitchen and bowing his head and saying the blessing." That conjunctive sentence presents a vivid scene, solid details, and a refreshing evocative phrase: "peppermint morning." Parris goes on to tell us some of the things Grandma made in her kitchen, "for she wasn't one to have any truck with storebought stuff" or "one for wasting time with cookbooks": "Grandma cooked by rule of finger—a pinch of this and a dab of that. Her taste buds were sharp and she humored them, and nobody ever fussed with her likes."

Mountain Cooking is a homecoming table groaning with John Parris's likes: His taste buds are sharp, and he humors them, and we enjoy the results. A Sylva native, he worked for United Press International and the Associated Press in New York and London before return-ing to the hills after World War II and writing his appreciations of self-reliant and inventive fellow mountaineers, characters praised by Wolfe (himself a far-flung Appalachian rambler) as "rugged, provin-cial, intelligent, and industrious." How happy the former diplomatic correspondent must have been to visit Mrs. Florence Alexander of Sandy Mush and taste what she put before him: "The pie was hot and golden, with a roof on it, and the sourwood honey had the look of liquid sunshine." What a fine day, when savoring "a lavish of sawmill gravy" at Phillips Restaurant in Robbinsville, to have Mrs. Phillips say: "Folks around here in the old days used to call it 'Life Everlasting,' because, they said, it saved so many people's lives. [That gravy] was just about all they had to eat. They made a meal on it and cat-head biscuits." What a pleasure, when writing about huckle-berry johnnycake, to recall this colorful detail: "Back in grandpa's day, when it was huckleberryin' time in the hills, you could tell the ages of the children by the blue rings around their legs."

Though this book can be unabashedly sentimental, Parris is aware of the bittersweet nature of cooking and eating, of the shadows un-derlying traditional foodways. "Hog killing time is a hard time and a busy time for the womenfolks," he starts "Souse Meat and Liver Mush." He knows most cooks are women, and he knows how hard they must work to put food in mouths: "Most of a day went into the making," he says about cooking apple butter in a big kettle over a fire outdoors. "To many a mountain woman who grew up at a time when the kitchen stove occupied most of her sixteen-hour-long day, pickling is a heap sight more than just preparing cucumbers." Even a cozy sentence like "The hearth was the center of the home—the source of warmth, sometimes light, and always food" reminds us who tended that warmth and light, who prepared that food, and whose determined work kept the home's heart going. "The Winds of Thanksgiving," set in Webster, begins:

The winds of Thanksgiving always blew toward the big white house that used to sit back from the river here.

Once a year they whistled up the clan, calling the kin back from city and town and the hills around.

There was the pull of family in them, the yearning of kin to be with kin.

A lovely set-up, on the surface—over the river and through the woods, etc.—but notice that the house is now gone, that the family was scattered even then, that this happened only once a year. *Mountain Cooking* is shot through with yearning, with a hunger for long-gone family and friends and traditions, embodied in their food. The ending of "How an Apple Pie Assisted Cupid," about the last days of Parris's grandfather's life, when he could no longer eat the hot apple pie his wife made for him—pie that had convinced him to marry her, pie that he'd enjoyed for breakfast every day for sixty years—is deeply moving: "My mother always said Grandma died of a broken heart, just grieved herself into the grave for Grandpa."

Mountain Cooking is a heartfelt elegy for waning or vanishing traditional culture. It echoes the high lonesome bluegrass sound, each piece and recipe a sweetly melancholic song. "Now they belong to memory and a vanished past," he writes about molasses pullings, but that pronoun applies to most of the people and food in the book. "The years have drifted," as he concludes the final column. "The family circle has dwindled. Uncle Jake is gone. So are Uncle Jesse and Uncle Lee and Aunt Lou and Uncle John and Grandpa and Grandma." As Ralph Stanley sings in "Little Birdy": *A short time to stay here, a long time to be gone.*

But this book brings the community circles back together. So many of the dishes herein involved group efforts, not just the familiar quilting bees but also collective activities like blackberrying, bean-stringing, corn-shucking, apple-paring, candy-pulling, roof-raising, and rail-splitting. Though folks in old-time Appalachia may have been "Independent as All Git-Out," in the title of one piece, they were also helpful social beings who enjoyed doing things together. That is one of the pleasures of this book, to be reminded of such connectedness.

Another pleasure: All the food-related folklore and stories. We hear about "the Vanished Berry Peddlers" and "the month of the Green-corn Moon" and the use of chickens as currency at the country store. We learn how the odor of sassafras "is reputed to drive away bed-bugs," and how strawberries not only fed John the Baptist but also remove freckles, "cool the liver," and cure venereal infections. We meet Rufus Brevard Monteith, "the king of the mountain sorghum boilers." We meet Mrs. Tlitha Messter, who declares that an empty hornets' nest "makes the finest place in the world to store hen eggs in the wintertime. Keeps 'em from freezin'."

Sometimes *Mountain Cooking* reminds me of *Paul Green's Wordbook: An Alphabet of Reminiscence*, another working writer's collection of dis-appearing folkways embodied in language. This book, like Green's, preserves juicy historical dishes and serves them up, in cultural con-text. Infare supper. Rye coffee. Peartening juice. Cherry bounce. Gritted bread. Poke sallet. A mess of leatherbritches. Clay peas. A good bait of ramps. Hog and hominy. A gill of honey. Blackberry larrup. Mountain banana (pawpaw). Fried dried-apple pies:

> "They were all the go when I was coming on," Aunt Tennie Cloer said. "A sight more common than baked pies. Folks la-bored and throve on 'em.
>
> "Made 'em in the shape of a half moon and fried 'em in an iron skillet. Everybody called 'em half-moon pies. . . .
>
> "Mama would pack 'em in a hollow gum or a lard can and the menfolks would help themselves."

I love the image of those working men taking a break to lift those treats out of a section of black-gum trunk, lined with paper and filled with half-moon pies by someone who knew they needed and would enjoy them. "Everybody helped everybody else," she said. "They were accommodating times."

The recipes at the back of the book are fairly minimal on directions; this is not really a cookbook, as such. But if you're game, and willing to fill in the blanks, you could try your hand at Poor Man's Fried Chicken (fatback), Bear and Dumplings, Possum and Sweet Potatoes, Baked Groundhog ("NOTE: In the old days, the fat from the last cooking water and the baking pan was kept and was taken as a medicine for croup. Called groundhog oil, it was a highly regarded remedy"), Methodist Pie, Blackberry Flummery, Peach Leather, Stella's Universal Pickle, or Metheglin (mead). And one of these "recipes" brought my father to mind:

Cornbread and Milk

Fill a glass two-thirds full with cold sweet milk and crumble in pieces of hot or cold cornbread. Eat with a long-handled spoon. *Note:* Some fill the glass with broken pieces of cornbread and pour the milk over it. But either way, this has been a favorite one-dish supper for mountain folks since time out of mind.

My father ate this, with an iced-teaspoon, using buttermilk, which made me gag. But I'd never considered: Why did he eat it, whenever possible, with such relish? What times, happy or hard, was he remembering, from his growing up on Arlington Street in Asheville without a father, or from his time in the orphanage in Sylva with his two brothers? Might he have crossed paths with John Parris there, when they were hungry teenagers, in the early 1930s? I'll never know.

Are there shortcomings to *Mountain Cooking*? Of course, as there would be with most books published nearly four decades ago, collecting columns that go back to the mid-1950s. The foodways presented here are mighty WASPy, though we do get stories about Cherokee cookery, such as yellowjacket soup or disquani bread. One suspects that the extended quoted dialogue in many stories could not possibly be verbatim, though it does resemble colorful old-time mountain speech. And there is inevitable repetition, of story structure (often circular), but also of material and phrases, like *Law, me!*

Even so, Parris is a sympathetic listener, never condescending to his subjects or poking his cosmopolitan nose into a scene, despite the fact that one of his best friends is the chef at the Waldorf-Astoria. He loves and respects these mountaineers, and does not present them and their cooking in stereotypically *hillbilly* ways. Maybe I was pre-disposed to like him and his stories, since my mother did (I recently found an envelope stuffed full of yellowed "Roaming the Moun-tains" clippings). Maybe I've made him into the kindly grandfather I never had, and forgive him more than I should. Maybe, now that I'm approaching the hoary upcountry of senior citizenship, I'm more drawn to his genial garrulous retrospective mode. But I think his columns, corny and formulaic as they sometimes are, perform a valu-able service to his native region, saving distinctive ingredients that might otherwise have been lost and making a savory verbal meal of them. *Mountain Cooking* makes the Appalachian past intensely present to us, through the everlasting communion of food.

"A smidgen is a little," John Parris reminds us, "but a slue is a lot, and it might be a lavish or in some cases a God's plenty." This book, his last, is a feast, a God's plenty of how his and my hungry unfancy tenacious ancestors cooked, and ate, and talked, and pleasured their palates.

MICHAEL McFEE has published fourteen books. The most recent, *That Was Oasis* (Carnegie Mellon University Press), is his eighth full-length collection of poetry, and concludes with "McCormick Field," which was featured in Eno Publishers' *27 Views of Asheville*. An Asheville na-tive, he has taught in the Creative Writing Program at the University of North Carolina at Chapel Hill for several decades.

Garden Gate

※ ZELDA LOCKHART ※

IT MIGHT TAKE some sweet time, but I was going to build myself a garden fence to keep the deer out of the quarter acre I planned to till and plant and harvest. It was my first spring since returning down South, back home after living under the gray, colorless winters of a New York state sky. I moved to N.C. to find a piece of land, learn how to grow vegetables, and farm the way my grandparents did.

The line of trees just beyond the fruit trees on my land felt to me like somebody had planted down there before. Just below a perfect line of apple, pear, and fig trees was a field where nothing but milkweed grew. It was familiar in my blood, my home, the South. While I was tilling the soil, I could taste the sweet corn like my grandeddy grew. I fantasized that I would find arrowheads, then took back that fantasy since it would mean that I was fantasizing retrospective war. I enjoyed the dirt beneath my nails.

Lesson One: Most vegetables won't grow in red clay. I found an organic gardening book at Barnes & Noble and decided the next step was building an eco-friendly low-impact fence. The book said to take materials from your environment to use. So, I looked up at the tall bamboo that was springing fiddle-headed shoots every day. It would need to be cut back to keep it from walking its tall green legs across the whole land. I also considered the beautiful wisteria that dripped purple flowers, but choked the bamboo, the pine, and the poplar trees. A bamboo and wisteria fence. It was right there in the book. Low-impact. They said get your poles cut so that on a rainy day, when the soil is wet, they sink without hammering, then weave the wisteria between the sunken poles once the earth dries.

Each day, when it was time for the nap that my toddler no longer took, I let her make a pallet on the living room floor to watch *Clifford* and *Curious George*. From there she could see out the front door and through the screen porch to where I was working just beyond the trunks of the fruit trees. I'd have an hour each day to cut the poles Amish-style; I took my pruners and hacksaw and was able to make about ten poles a day including chopping off the bamboo branches. Brutal work, that no self-respecting New Yorker would ever praise me for. Wobbly armed and determined, I returned each day. To save time on rainy days, though, I still cut poles down, and I went ahead and began to sink some of them into the ground. I would reach up in the rain as high as my two hands could go up the chalky green bamboo poles and let both feet leave the ground, so all 160 of my pounds could sink the poles.

Often, rocks beneath the soil prevented the poles from sinking no matter how much weight was applied. Digging up rocks was taking too long, so I decided that the fence could be zigzag and that would be okay. Some days, with rain dripping into my eyes, I'd try to get in a little extra time, but the end of the *Curious George* theme song would signal my daughter's universal holler, "Mom, Mom." The red mud was so thick on my boots that I walked like I was wearing high heels back to the house.

Two months later, I finished the fence on the last day to plant (according to those yellow, orange, and red wavy lines across the U.S. on the back of my seed packs). The fence was impressive, if I may say so myself. It did not rock to the touch, was more than eight feet tall, and from the house was a striking structure in the distance, a fort around the whole quarter acre of vegetable garden, or rather tilled soil, or rather seeded red mud. I had even been clever enough to build an overlap maze at the opening because the book said no need for latches, the deer will not figure out how to walk in via an overlapping view of poles.

Planting, weeding, that sun. Damn! Where did sun this hot come from? Was it hotter than when I was a child playing hide-and-seek behind my grandfather's hay rolls? After the first few weeks I felt that this endeavor made me either a genius or a fool. I dropped five pounds of water weight by sweating into the soil while trying to keep the weeds back enough for the seeds to come up. Every day I felt closer to the fool end of the spectrum.

I finished writing my novel, *Cold Running Creek,* that summer, because I knew what it felt like to be an American slave. At the end of the day, my arms were rubber bands while I made dinner for my daughter. "Soon," I told her, "we'll have vegetables from there."

The mustard greens came up first and were prolific. The herbs never showed up even after I turned compost into the soil. But then came the only other vegetable ornery enough to grow in clay: corn. I turned my full attention to those stalks. There was something religious about a plant that reached for the sun like that and bore fruit. Each day, I oiled the silk to keep the worms away, I pulled the weeds away, and played in my imagination like I was the boy in *Sounder,* running through the cornstalks.

In *Cold Running Creek* I wrote the scene of Lilly on her horse doing what I wanted, riding through the rows. Though my rows of corn were short, in my mind they were miles long, and in my heart the tall green and gold reaching to the blue sky was connecting me to my ancestors. Some days while I gardened, I stepped outside my garden gate with my toddler in hand and squatted to pee. We were home indeed, and were going to be adding corn to the table treasures that made us wild. Even my hair, ignored by my busy gardening hands, had grown into wild tendrils.

The night before the corn would be picked, my daughter and my two neighbors and I sat at the fire circle and sang and even howled to solidify the lost boy fairy-tale moment.

That night, the light from the moon brushed its slow hand over the top of my head in affirmation, the way a parent caresses the head of her sleeping child, but I did not know that she was soothing me before the next lesson.

Lesson Two: Low impact yields to high impact. In the morning I took the old laundry basket to fill with corn, took the spirit stick I'd made so the glass eye on the stick could bear witness for my ancestors of what I'd learned to do.

As I approached the garden fort, something didn't look right, something looked too much like the days of emptiness and disjointedness when I was building the fence. And there, in the middle of the trampled mess that was once my garden a buck and his herd. His antlers had pushed down the fence to show his family where I had created for them a feast. I screamed, roared really, and entered the rink ready, swinging the spirit stick; of course I was not thinking of my ancestors anymore. My feet were not quite on the ground when the anger in the top of my head lifted me as I ran toward him; a battle approach that stopped when he blew through his nostrils and stomped the ground and I smelled his musty body. There we stood, and I didn't question my foolishness. All I could do was be still and let the anger leave the top of my head and stream down my face in tears where I stood in the piles of silk and shucks of my labor. The fence leaned in reverence to the buck who turned and walked away, his big haunches switching in a kiss-my-ass sort of fashion.

Lesson Three: There are rural gangsters, the deer, who will wait for you to work your ass off and steal you blind.

The next March, the last frost lifted and reminded me that the hottest place on our land was the backyard. It was fenced with an eight-foot, non-Amish, high-impact fence with wire mesh around the bottom, bolted locks and joints. I had decided when I moved here that, with a propane tank there and wire attached to the fence, the backyard was aesthetically wrong for a garden. But it had been almost two years since we'd left the gray, cold skies of N.Y. state, so fashion was less my concern. Hell, by then I even smelled a little like my Mississippi grandeddy.

I took my tools to that fenced-in space, and my daughter and I tilled, planted, harvested. We ate hearty from the backyard that summer: watermelon, cantaloupe, kale, collards, pole beans, edamame, blackberries, and all the herbs we could manage to grow. My daughter and I looked like we had chlorophyll in our blood. We were electric brown with the light on beneath our skin.

The fruit trees? Well, I learned to "break off a piece of the action" for the deer so that we could live peacefully in the same neighborhood. The high fruit is mine, the low fruit is theirs.

ZELDA LOCKHART is author of *Fifth Born*, a Barnes & Noble Discovery selection, *Cold Running Creek*, winner of an Honor Fiction Award from the Black Caucus of the American Library Association, and *Fifth Born II: The Hundredth Turtle*, a finalist for a Lambda Literary Foundation Award. Her prose and poetry appear in periodicals like *Chautauqua*, *Obsidian II*, and *USAToday.com*. She is currently pursuing a PhD in Expressive Art Therapies.

Make It Holy

Challah, *Chicken Marbella, and My Sabbath Tribe*

☀ RICHARD CHESS ☀

MOCK CHOPPED LIVER. (Ashkenazic, adapted.)

Baruch Atah, Adonai Eloheinu, Melech haolam, hazan et haolam kulo b'tuvo . . ./Sovereign of the universe, we praise You: Your goodness feeds/ sustains the world.

Salted pistachio nuts. (Persian.)

. . . *hazan et haolam kulo b'tuvo, b'chein b'chesed u'v'rachamim/*feeds/ sustains the world with grace, love, and compassion.

Rahamim: a Hebrew word related to *rehem*, the Hebrew word for womb. In its mother's womb, the fetus is fed and sustained. It neither deserves nor does not deserve the nutrients, the sustenance it receives. Sustained on grace and love, it develops and grows.

Hickory smoked trout on Ak-Mak sesame crackers. (Trout: American, Sunburst Farms, Shining Rock Wilderness in Pisgah National Forest; crackers: Armenian.)

I, too, am fed. I, too, am sustained. But I earned it, right, this food? Six days I labored. I graded, I conferenced, I annotated, I printed. I dry-marked a smart board and deleted or saved. I suffered while others slept. Unrested, unhappy, I rose six mornings to the alarm of another day. I deserve these appetizers.

Salsa made of homegrown tomatoes and cilantro. (Salsa: Mayan; tomatoes: Central American; cilantro: Levantine, though these tomatoes and cilantro were grown in a garden on Westchester Drive, Asheville, North Carolina.) Spanish olives.

I earned it, right, this double portion of food and family and friends, this *gift* of Friday night?

These talented, accomplished, loyal, loving friends: I earned them, right? Because I'm a good listener, they are mine to keep, right? Shabbat after Shabbat after Shabbat, I am received by them in their homes and they are received by my wife and me in ours. *Bo-i v'shalom . . . gam b'simchah uv'tzoholah; bo-i, bo-i/* enter in peace, gladness, and joy. Those are the words with which Jews in synagogue welcome the Sabbath. Though we are not in synagogue, and though we do not sing this hymn in our homes, that's the spirit with which we welcome each other, our Sabbath regulars, our Sabbath tribe, at the end of a long week.

But sometimes I wonder, what have I done to deserve them, what do I have to offer them, these friends of decades of Sabbaths together? I cannot diagnose disease, I have barely a child's grasp of the law, I do not have a business plan, I don't dice or season, bake or grill, I cannot stitch or fiddle or lift, I have not saved a forest, I rarely see and call out privilege, I am not generous with my body, my secrets, my time.

Hu notein lechem l'chol basar / Source of bread for all who live.

Challah: Sabbath and holiday bread; braided strands of truth, justice, peace.

I am alive; I live. After lighting candles, after blessing children, our daughters and sons now scattered about the country, and after blessing their sons and daughters, those of our grown kids who have kids of their own, after *kiddush*, the blessing of wine that invites us to recall the beginning of creation *and* the redemption from slavery, the lifting of our ancestors free of that narrow place called *Mitzrayim/* Egypt, comes the bread.

Fourth in this line of rituals, the *challah* is covered until its time arrives to be revealed in the light of blessing. Some say it is covered as a reminder of the dew that covered and preserved the manna that fed the Hebrews wandering through the desert. Some say it is covered so it will not feel slighted by the attention paid to the candles, children, and wine. Some say its covering is like the bride's veil. Shabbat, in Jewish lore, is likened to a bride. I think its unveiling reminds us that it's our responsibility to uncover truth, justice, and peace, which often seem buried under lies, injustice, and conflict. Shabbat comes around every seven days to remind us.

Our Shabbat tribe's custom is that the youngest among us has the honor of leading the *motzi*, the blessing over the bread. These days, when our children are rarely in town to celebrate Shabbat with us, that means the one among us in his or her early sixties. She or he reveals the *challah* and with both hands lifts it and leads us in singing the blessing of thanks after which we pass the loaf around, each tearing off a piece.

Challah. (Torah, Numbers 15:18–21, but this never egg-y enough *challah* is baked at Annie's, Asheville, North Carolina.)

The Friday night bread on which I am sustained in Asheville is the bread on which I've been sustained on many Friday nights elsewhere—Gainesville, Florida; Jerusalem and Safed, Israel; New Rochelle, New York; Simi Valley, California; Cherry Hill, New Jersey. Wherever I happen to be standing as Shabbat arrives, whoever I happen to be, withdrawn or engaged, from one Friday evening to the next, the Shabbat I receive is Shabbat, and the source of Shabbat is the Source, and the Source crosses geographic, state, and national borders, party affiliation, culinary difference, identity and mood confusion and evolution.

The bread I receive from the Source of all on Friday night is the bread of friendship.

Then Chicken Marbella (Sephardic—Morocco and Spain) and green beans (United States) sautéed in olive oil (ancient Syria) and garlic (Central Asia, though this garlic is locally grown).

Then blackberry crumble. (North America.)

Then *Birkat Hamazon*, Grace After Meals, passages of which have been threading through this meditation.

When we chant it, one of my favorite prayers, I remember to notice the taste of butternut squash or chickpea stew on farro or grilled salmon lingering in my mouth, or blackberries and vanilla ice cream, and I experience squash as squash, blackberry as blackberry. But, at the instant word meets physical sensation, I also experience, as deeply as I've ever experienced anything, the delicious taste of love and goodness. Fed and nourished by creation and the Source of all creation, my physical and spiritual hunger abated for now, I am wholly satisfied.

A Sabbath meal is not a meal without a text, read aloud, chanted, sung.

But we almost never sing it, my holy Sabbath friends and I. (Holy: the first time the word is used in Torah is in Genesis when God calls the Sabbath *holy*.)

Without a final prayer, we hug and kiss each other *Shabbat Shalom* (*Shabbat*: Sabbath; *shalom*: peace, wholeness) then turn away from each other for the night, each of us living her and his own story of what makes us peaceful, whole, and holy.

RICHARD CHESS has lived in Asheville since 1989. He is the author of three books of poetry, *Tekiah, Chair in the Desert,* and *Third Temple.* His work has appeared in many publications, including *Best American Spiritual Writing 2005* and *Telling and Remembering: A Century of America Jewish Poetry.* He is a regular contributor to *Good Letters: The Image Blog.* He directs University of North Carolina at Asheville's Center for Jewish Studies and chairs the Department of English.

On Food and Other Weapons

※ DIYA ABDO ※

FOOD IS HER only currency.

She has nothing else to offer me, she thinks. No other means by which to tempt me.

"I want to tell you about how hard it has been for me. . . . I, too, am a refugee. Won't you scurry around for me as you do for the others? I have things I want you to know. . . . Come. Visit me, please. I will make you a delicious meal."

In Jordan, thousands of miles from the Glen Haven Apartments[1] in Greensboro where this Iraqi refugee woman now lives, my Palestinian refugee grandmother would do the same. "Diya, my love. Come visit me, my darling. I will make you a *maqloobeh*.[2] By God, its deliciousness will be one you've never tasted before."

When I became a vegetarian, her purse-belt took a real hit. But she adjusted quickly, still making stuffed grape leaves and zucchini, now with extra tomatoes and parsley instead of ground meat.

What other currency does an illiterate refugee woman
have—when she is divorced or her husband is an invalid,
when her children are grown and gone or young and

---

1. Low-income housing in Greensboro with a high refugee population.

2. *Maqloobeh* translates to Upside Down, a one-pot rice dish with meat and vegetables on the bottom, but they end up on top after the dish is cooked and turned upside down out of the pot onto the serving dish.

dependent—but the olive oil at the bottom of her pot,
     soaking into the grains of rice as it simmers,
in the badly equipped kitchen,
in the dirty ghetto,
in the second or third or fourth never-a-home host country?

For me, it was never and always about the food, *ya teita*.[3]

☀   ☀   ☀

THEY TRAVEL IN my mother's luggage across the Atlantic like little weapons—the latest in zucchini hollowing technology. She presents me with the two vegetable corers, very proudly. They look dangerous and highly ineffective—green-handled, spindly thin rod with a sharp small circle at the tip.

At the Super G Mart, I make the ritual search for the smallest sage-green, fuzzy-yellow-striped zucchini. Moving around the thicker, longer ones from the top, I rummage through the pile and find a few I can use. The big ones don't work as well; they need a lot of the rice mixture (extra tomatoes and parsley) to fill them up. The rice rarely cooks through, and if I wait until it does, the zucchini will have turned to mush. With the big ones, you have to sacrifice one part of the meal for the other—the vessel for its passengers or the visitors for the host.

The small zucchini absolves me from that compromise.

☀   ☀   ☀

MY LITTLEST, SEIRA, loves coring the zucchini with me.

And even though she's only two, and the tip of that toy-like green handle as sharp as a razor, I let her.

Instinctively, it seems, she knows how to handle it. Slowly, she sticks the circle into the top of the zucchini, its crown decapitated,

---

3. *Teita*" is "grandmother" in Levantine Arabic. *Ya* functions like the "Oh" in an address, only informal.

and twists her arm. She wants to be able to do what I do—pull out the magic wand and spill out the bowels, ribbons of butter-yellow pulp, into the trash. My oldest, Aidana, would rather fill the now disemboweled cylinders. The salty, savory, olive-oily rice mixture drips down her wrist and forearm as she stuffs them through the narrow opening. All she wants to do, really, is lick her fingers and eat the raw rice. After soaking in hot water and then marinating in spices, it is toothsome and delicious.

Once cooked, she won't have anything to do with it.

But she loves freekeh, the ancient grain. And when she asks me to make it, I know it's because she wants to help me "clean" it. Spreading a cupful out in a wide pan, she fans her fingers through the husky grains, looking for the tiny stones.

"Is this one?"

"No, that's freekeh"

"Are you sure? It's really hard."

"Yes, but it won't be when it's cooked."

"See, this little gray thing. This." It's round, like a little bullet, only much smaller. "You have to be patient to find all of them."

Cleaning freekeh takes time—slow methodical sectioning of the grains, inspecting each section carefully for the stow-away pellets.

You don't want your teeth to find them once the freekeh is cooked, I tell her. They can easily break on the unexpected solid speck in the mouthful of creamy porridge.

❊　❊　❊

IN THEIR TEMPORARY house, nestled in the woods of Guilford College, just beyond the lake, the Syrian refugee family we are hosting[4] wait for their daily visitors—a pair of Muscovy ducks. These are border-crossing birds, originally from South America. And though

---

4. The family was hosted as part of Every Campus a Refuge, a Guilford-founded initiative that advocates for housing refugees on campus grounds and assisting them in resettlement. This family has since "graduated" from the program and moved off campus.

tropical, these two have made their home in the cooler climes of North Carolina. Moored to the Guilford lake, they have found refuge in the surrounding homes and humans.

The pair waddle hurriedly toward the front porch.

The mother sees them first. Her turn now to walk awkwardly, limping quickly toward the door. She shouts out to the father: "I have rice ready for them." He smiles at me with incredulous joy, his eyes always on the verge of tears. "Ya Diya, they come every day at this time. Three p.m. Can you imagine?"

Yes, I can. Please. Come visit me. I will feed you.

"They eat everything we give them—rice with meat, lentil soup, soaked bread."

The father squats on the stoop, smoking his cigarette, looking at the ducks, and communing with them in the guzzling, gulping silence.

＊   ＊   ＊

DO SWANS GRIEVE?

Circling the little cygnet, the mother swan is magnetized to, but does not look directly at, the bobbing mound of feathers. The cygnet's head and neck are in the water. The mother lowers her own neck to drink little gulps, always near the baby. The father makes his aggressive pilgrimage back and forth between the dead cygnet and the mother and the fenced edge of the pond, his wings tense, his neck stretched back.

But for the death, there is no sadness here. It is the suggestion of mourning—the unnerving restraint, the tearless circling, the seething back and forth—that devastates.

How did Seira, two years old and always in motion, know to sit there on the bench, still, in utter silence for so many minutes? Something about the swan's circling, her unthirsty drinking, told her this was a time for grieving.

The keeper of the swans, the man who owns Jim King's Pond in the wealthy Greensboro neighborhood of Hamilton Lakes and whose house is right next door, tells us that there might not be enough food. The swans and the turtles are fighting for what is there. Perhaps that is why the turtles are killing the cygnets—they are trying to eat them.

He plans to trap and kill all the turtles. "Thir gittin' ma swans."

The vessel for the passengers.

Visit me every year—if only once.
Just please don't forget me altogether. . . .
Fairuz[5] begs over the airwaves.

The Syrian mother rolls cabbage and grape leaves for the gathering. They are thin and long—a testament to her skills. My grandmother used to say that a rolled grape leaf should be no larger than a grown woman's pinky.

I look at my little finger and think about that untenable expectation, made even more impossible by the solitary living of a refugee woman's first arrival. Pinky-sized stuffed grape leaves require much time; they assume the communal living of women gathered in a bare kitchen—grandmothers, daughters, granddaughters—circling the tray of leaves, snatching one, placing it on the left palm, quickly pinching the rice, centering the grains on the leaf and then molding them into a narrow tube, deftly folding the sides and rolling the leaf rapidly.

But the mother cooks her feast unassisted. "May my swollen wrists bear witness on my behalf," she boasts. The leaves aren't piled high the way they would have been had her girls been with her, but they are sufficiently slim. Next to the leaves, on the coffee tables pulled together, she has artfully arranged the other dishes she's prepared: stuffed zucchini, *muttabal*[6] and hummus, the minty salad she knows I love, freekeh, fried *kebbeh*,[7] lentil soup. We gather round, a motley-bale of first-generation refugees (from Syria, Palestine, Afghanistan). Huddled round the food, shoulder to shoulder, arms extended, we

5. A very famous Lebanese singer beloved by Arabs pan-nationally.
6. Eggplant dip.
7. The Arab version of the meat samosa made with bulgur.

look like the lake-turtles in their basking—rim to rim, necks out-stretched, each for its own morsel of the sun. The Afghani boys have no Arabic and the mother has no English. They tell me to "tell her that her food is delicious." That it tastes exactly like something they eat in Afghanistan. She smiles at their compliment shyly, proudly. She extends her wrists again in testament. *Ahlan wa sahlan.* You are welcome here.

And eat, she insists. Eat more. There is always enough food for all the friends who enter here, including the ducks. No compromises. No fear. The zucchinis are just the right size, the dangerous cooking utensils have been put away, the stow-away stones in the freekeh found.

The food is ready, delicious, safe.

Only please. Come visit me.

DIYA ABDO is a first-generation Palestinian, born and raised in Jordan. Currently an associate professor of English and chair of the Department of English and Creative Writing at Guilford College, she teaches and writes about Arab women writers and Arab and Islamic feminisms. She has published poetry, fiction, and creative nonfiction, and is a contributor to Eno's *27 Views of Greensboro.* Her public essays focus on the intersection of gender, political identity, and vocation. She is the founder and director of Every Campus a Refuge. Guilford has hosted two Syrian families and a Ugandan thus far.

Lessons in Table Manners and Life

❊ HEATHER NEWTON ❊

WHEN I WAS a child growing up in Raleigh, my family had a tradition of inviting one or two friends to join us for dinner at the Plantation Inn every Christmas season. The Plantation Inn was a fancy restaurant attached to a less fancy motel. It had never been part of an actual plantation but it looked very Old South—all white with antebellum columns. Inside, the carpet was lush and red and candy canes hung from the chandeliers. A lady in an evening gown played Christmas carols on an electric organ in the corner. To my child eyes the Plantation Inn epitomized elegance.

To understand the significance of this annual event you must know that with four children and not much discretionary income, my family almost never went out to eat. When we did, we went to IHOP, or if Burger King had Whoppers on sale for a quarter my dad might spring for a bag. Otherwise, we ate at home. The local paper even did a full-page feature on my mother in which she proudly gave tips about how to feed a family of six on twenty-five dollars a week.

My parents' intent in starting the Plantation Inn tradition was to honor the friends we took as guests, and to teach us children how to behave in public. Going to the Plantation Inn was a big deal. We dressed up. We hung our coats in a cloak closet as we entered. The tables were set with something called "cloth napkins." Our parents expected us to chew with our mouths closed, refrain from licking our plates and, for one sweet evening, stop hitting each other.

Their efforts to turn us into ladies and gentlemen succeeded during the meal, but always fell apart when it was time to leave because of one thing—the mint bowl. On a coffee table in the lobby sat an oblong silver serving dish full of butter mints. The idea, of course, was for patrons to take one mint to cleanse their palates after dinner. Because my mother's food budget didn't allow for candy at home, however, my siblings and I had no self-control whatsoever when we encountered candy elsewhere. Every year we stuffed handfuls of mints into our mouths and our linty pockets, completely cleaning out the bowl.

One fateful year as my dad was settling the check, another little girl sat on the couch in the lobby, surreptitiously raiding the mint bowl. As we watched, she reached out and somehow hit one end of the candy dish, flipping it high in the air. Pastel-colored mints rained down and the dish landed upside-down on the floor. Oh, the humanity. The hostess rushed over and swept all the mints into the trash. My siblings and I lingered as long as we could by the cloak closet hoping the hostess would refill the bowl, but she never did. As long as we live we will never forgive that clumsy little girl.

The guests we invited to the Plantation Inn included close family friends and people my parents wanted to know better. A few were couples but most were single. They were teachers, writers, a minister, a wood carver. My favorite was a young man who had served as a missionary in Kenya. He spoke a made-up language called "Alfalfa" (similar to Pig Latin, only funnier). When he told a story in Alfalfa my normally reserved father laughed so hard tears spurted from his eyes. The trait all our guests shared was that they were *interesting* and willing to engage with grownups and children alike. They entertained me and they listened to me.

In his book *Confederates in the Attic*, Tony Horwitz describes the Plantation Inn as "a faux plantation motel on a busy suburban road, right across from Kmart" where a group "designed to prepare youngsters for Confederate citizenship" had decided to have its annual meeting. For me, despite its politically incorrect name, the Plantation Inn was not a nostalgic symbol of the fallen South. I remember how warm and cozy it always was, the savory smells that rose from silver chafing dishes on the buffet line, the strong hands of the man who carved the roast beef, his uniform and chef's hat as crisp and white as the snow we never got for Christmas in North Carolina. And I remember the lessons I learned there: Treasure your friends, old and new. Show them you value them. Enjoy them.

HEATHER NEWTON's novel, *Under the Mercy Trees*, won the Thomas Wolfe Memorial Literary Award, was chosen by the Women's National Book Association as a Great Group Reads Selection, and was an Okra Pick by the Southern Independent Booksellers Alliance. Her short fiction has appeared in *The Drum, 27 Views of Asheville, Crucible,* and elsewhere. She teaches creative writing for the University of North Carolina at Asheville's Great Smokies Writing Program. Her Asheville law practice focuses on employment law and business advice for writers, artists, and entrepreneurs.

The Pies That Bind

☀ STEVEN PETROW ☀

MY WINNING STREAK as our family's champion pie king ended several years ago—that's when all the trouble started. Since going to college in the Old North State, I'd sat on the holiday pie throne without fear of challenge, learning early what my Hillsborough neighbor Frances Mayes wrote with great authority in *Under the Tuscan Sun*, "[P]ecan pie [is] a necessary ingredient of Christmas." Remaining the king was a result of the time I'd invested refining my pecan pie recipe—which, if I may—had two outstanding attributes: a generous helping of Kentucky bourbon to cut the treacly sweetness of the Karo Syrup and a top-secret mixing technique that prevented the pie from becoming gelatinous.

Perfection! And no one dared bring another pecan pie to our family's Christmas table.

Until 2007, that is, which just happened to be the year I turned fifty. That year, my sister's wife, Maddy, invited Megan, a new and much younger sister-in-law of hers, to our family table. Just married, beautiful, and eight months pregnant, how could we not embrace her? It was all air kisses and *mwah*s, until Megan murmured, "I brought a pecan pie. . . ."

At that very moment, I knew Maddy had betrayed me. I mean, how could she have failed to disclose to Megan, "Oh, only Steven makes the pecan pie in this family." She might also have added that my pies had seen us through our family's ups and downs—from the death of my grandmother (who was known to stick her fork right into the uncut pie and start eating) to the birth of three nieces and a nephew (each celebrated with a pie). Every holiday season, we consumed a delicious slice of family history along with our calories.

All too soon came dessert, and for the first time in our family we faced two pecan pies on the sideboard—mine crafted with the aforementioned bourbon and a dollop of entitlement, and Megan's with a dash of bravado and another of comeuppance.

As we raised fork to mouth, Megan launched into a long yarn about how her "heirloom pecans" came from her great-godmother in Lamar, Mo. "Every year she hand-picked them, hand-shelled them, and then sent them to me. The magic of her pecans is part of what makes this pie so delicious!" showing absolutely no consideration for her treasonous presence. Then, she explained how this year, in her third trimester, she'd gone to the farm and climbed up a rickety ladder to harvest the nuts for this very pie. By the time she was finished, I knew I was finished. No matter how delicious my pie, Megan's family history was about to trump ours, with my very own flesh and blood ready to dethrone me.

And, yes, nearly every one of them voted against me; their forks enthusiastically awarding Megan, the outsider, our family's annual pecan pie accolade.

The following Christmas, I joined a new family myself, my now-husband's big, boisterous clan in Winston-Salem. His family, which came ready-made with several sisters-in-law, naturally had its own history and traditions. And it was Sister Lisa, at least a baker's dozen years younger than me, who owned the pecan pie trophy. Honestly, I didn't know about that when I offered to bring one of my own prize-winners to Christmas dinner, nor did my new mother-in-law warn me away from pecan to, say, pumpkin.

Still, I had learned a thing or two from Megan and her storytelling. And soon enough, Sister Lisa's pie and my own sat side-by-side on my mother-in-law's marble countertop, awaiting their comers. To be fair, Lisa's was a handsome pie, if not a tad untraditional—made with maple syrup, horrors!—instead of Karo. But it came *sans* story-line, without history.

By contrast, let me just say that the gathering of the pecans in my pie, from a mom and pop farm in Goldsboro, had a tale of woe like you've never imagined. It was Rabelais's *Gargantua and Pantagruel* all over again, and I told the farmers' story slowly and carefully: Famine, floods, and pestilence! Not to mention I mixed in my own family story, as a way of introducing myself to the new in-laws.

By dessert's end, the voting was in: My pie pan was empty, and poor Lisa went home with a good third of her humble pie.

Fast-forward to subsequent yuletide seasons, where *pecan pie* becomes a trending topic in our family just after Thanksgiving. As the Karo Syrup binds the nuts, so, too, the pie now does for my clan. Most years now Lisa sends me a "hugs and kisses" Facebook message in early December, ostensibly lamenting our missed visit at Thanksgiving but no doubt trying to decipher whether she or I will bring our prized pies to Mother Helen's (our shared mother-in-law) on Christmas Day. We've learned our lesson: Lisa and I don't ever bring our pies to the same gathering. In fact, she warned me last year: "I'm going to start a whole new tradition this year and make my Mama's nine-layer chocolate cake. That has a great story and no pecans!"

As for the larger lesson, well, that's pretty clear now: It's not about the bourbon, my secret mixing technique—not even the pedigree of the nuts. It's about the life of the pie—the traditions we mix up year after year that, with any luck, bind us together as family. For those of us in middle age, not only do we get to share our recipes, but our family history and stories, too, which seem only to get better with age. To paraphrase the yuletide story, "Happy Christmas to all, and to all a good bite."

Steven Petrow's Bourbon Pecan Pie

SERVES 8

1   cup dark Karo Syrup (no maple syrup!)

1   cup white granulated sugar

3   eggs

2   tablespoons unsalted butter, melted

¼   cup bourbon (you can use as little as 2 tablespoons if you prefer)

1   teaspoon almond extract

1½ to 1¾ cups   (about 6 to 7 ounces) whole pecans—the best and freshest you can find; learn as much about them as you can, whether from the farmer or the label

1   unbaked 9-inch deep pie crust (I will save the topic of making pie crusts for another time)

Preheat oven to 350°. Combine the Karo Syrup, sugar, eggs, melted butter, bourbon, and almond extract. Mix well.

Pay attention to this next crucial step: Fold in the pecans slowly, making sure they're evenly distributed throughout the filling. Do not over-mix.

Pour the mixture into the unbaked pie crust. With your fingers, arrange the topmost layer of pecans so that they lie flat, with the rounded side facing up (no need to become too obsessive). Bake for 55 to 60 minutes, until a toothpick inserted in the center comes out clean. Let sit for a couple of hours.

Meanwhile, start to talk up the story of your pecans to anyone who will listen.

Journalist STEVEN PETROW is the go-to guy on modern manners, and he's written five books on the subject. He writes the Civilities column for the *Washington Post*, as well as Digital Life for *USA Today*, and previously wrote the Civil Behavior column in the *New York Times*, and Digital Dilemmas for *Parade* magazine. He's working on a new book about illness, death, and dying. He lives in Hillsborough with his husband, Jim Bean.

Blue Monday

☀ JOHN McELWEE ☀

THE RIVER USED to boil here with fish in the spring. Thousands of shad, herring, striped bass, eels, even sturgeon, surged upstream from the Atlantic to spawn in their natal freshwater. In George Graham's lifetime, all but the shad have effectively disappeared after decades of overfishing, hydroelectric projects, pollution, and the introduction of ravenous non-native species like blue catfish. At sixty-eight, he's among the few remaining commercial fishermen on the Cape Fear River, one of North Carolina's main waterways.

The shad, George told me, were making a gradual comeback. "If I threw a net right now, I'd have me fifty fish before the bend," he said, pointing to where the water disappeared, a couple hundred yards away. "But the state cut the damn season short."

We stood on a lock and dam in East Arcadia, one of three built on the Cape Fear over a century ago to facilitate industrial navigation to Elizabethtown, Tar Heel, and Fayetteville, sixty-five miles upstream. We are speaking over the roar of a fish ladder, a river-wide staircase of massive stones, built recently to encourage migration.

From here the river rolls low, wide, and brown, spanned occasionally by rusty bridges, silly with oxbows and a miscellany of otter slides and abandoned fishing camps southeast for thirty-one miles. There it picks up the glassy, Guinness-colored Black River—the runoff from a series of coastal swamps that conceal the world's oldest bald cypress, a tree named Methuselah—and in twenty-two more miles arcs through the barge-clotted port of Wilmington, and out to the Big Water.

George grew up in a cabin on the banks, not far from the lock, fishing in hand-built boats, and says he can feel shad in the water. "I got fishing in my blood."

❁ ❁ ❁

IT WAS THE day after Easter, or as it's known around here, Blue Monday. On King's Bluff, a grassy shelf overlooking the lock and dam, a crowd of several hundred had gathered for the Blue Monday Shad Fry, an event celebrating the start of spring, and the shad runs that signal it.

I arrived early in East Arcadia, a confluence of long, straight roads along the spare, sun-border of Bladen and Columbus counties. The town itself is marked by a string of single-story homes, a garden in back of each, and a few shuttered small businesses—Blanks Grocery and the Party Lite convenience store persist—two churches, a one-room satellite campus of Bladen Community College. The small population comprises a cluster of African-American families descended from an isolated group of mixed-race free people and slaves from the adjoining Lloyd and Black Rock plantations, which dealt in timber and shad. Many of them have been in the area since the 1790s, and the current generation, whose forebears lived largely off the land and what the river could provide, work in a handful of nearby factories. The town ends at the river.

It was hot at ten in the morning on the bluff, and neon dogwood blossoms tipped winter-bare branches under a wide bright sky. Most of the old-timers wore blue T-shirts made for the occasion: *East Arcadia Blue Monday Fish Fry.* I bought a similarly marked hat. Cowboy boots abounded—"This is boot country," one man told me—and jerseys and tattoos were popular among the younger generation.

"Black, white, or brown, if you want to eat we'll feed you," Earl Brown, one of the event's organizers, told me repeatedly. A handful of thick-wristed men in denim and camouflage edged the bluff, eyes shaded with low hats. Dressed-up local politicians shook hands and asked for votes. A three-hundred-pound man in a purple suit handed me a postcard, featuring himself in a white suit, pointing, with a stern brow: *Newton for Sherriff: Qualify Your Vote.*

A churchly ceremony kicked off the day with a pastor's invocation, followed by Jimmy Gatlin, a one-time Grand Ole Opry singer, who crooned gospel to programmed Casio music. He kept it up, heroically, all day long. There was an ROTC color guard on hand, and a politician presented the community with a state flag, retired from the capitol. This year, for the first time, Blue Monday had been recognized by the state legislature as a holiday—an occasion of great pride for East Arcadians, who have a keen sense for historical preservation, in an area mostly known for Revolutionary and Civil War battle sites and plantation homes. The act made official one of several conflicting origin stories associated with the event: In the 1940s, local business owners Bernard Carter, Moses Blanks, and Archie and Chester Graham revived the regional tradition of frying the day after Easter. Over the years their gathering had grown to include the rest of the community and its diaspora up north. Younger generations have since taken up the torch. Their families assembled before the stage, parading children, grandchildren, and great-grandchildren, who restlessly toed the grass as the smell of frying batter leached sweetly into the air, mingling with the sweeter smell of bacon fat, and wafted into our faces by a breeze over the river. Finally, a line stretched across the bluff, and we prepared to eat.

* * *

GEORGE GRAHAM IS in charge of acquiring the shad. He learned to fish from his father, Archie, a riverbank sharecropper and seasonal factory worker who sold shad and catfish in the spring. George has reddish-brown skin and a high-pitched, lilting voice, which crackles with extra syllables in the local style. "When the owls holler, that's when I know I'm gonna catch me a fish," George told me. We were far enough Down East that the river was tidal—a shift announced, he confided, by the owls—and the shad run better at night. The state no longer allows nets in the water on weekends, ending George's forty-three-year practice of fishing following long weeks of working at the paper mill. So on weeknights leading up to the fry, George heads a handful of local fishermen who splay thirty-yard nets over the water, with corks every eight feet to mark their haul. Checking the corks and the bank with a spotlight at intervals, they drift in the quiet dark a few miles netting pounds of fish. They'd had to freeze the supply this year, George told me with a grimace, since the new season ended two weeks before Easter.

Preparation of shad varies regionally. In New England, where it's celebrated for keeping George Washington's troops alive at Valley Forge, the fish is traditionally planked: split in half and nailed skin-side down to oak or cedar planks, which are propped before coals and basted with pork fatback dangled from a switch. Other colonials cooked the fish on gridirons over hickory coals, or in rectangular boxes called roasting kitchens. Around here the custom has been to fry the shad in a long-handled cast-iron skillet. In the old days, Blue Monday participants cooked over barrel-and-cinderblock fires on the riverbank, on the land that George's father sharecropped. They occasionally resorted to fashioning fryers out of scrap metal—a setup that must have somewhat resembled today's rig, a three-by-four-foot welded steel skillet fryer over propane.

George and his friends steak the shad, cutting the meat perpendicular to the spine, and deep fry it in a light batter of meal, ground red pepper, and salt. The flesh is white and oily, crowded with translucent gray bones, and has a powerful, gamy flavor—the result of muscle depletion from their spawning runs, during which the hard-bodied creatures fast. You can taste the sea—the American shad's scientific name, *Alosa sapidissima,* translates aptly as "most savory."

As the line moved, I lingered in the cooking station, where a heavy-set man named Rico doled out hot fish on paper plates packed with homemade hushpuppies—ideal, I gathered, for pushing down stubborn, gullet-stuck bones—coleslaw, and baked beans. On an adjacent burner, Leonard Hall, a cousin and fishing partner of Graham's, husbanded a vat of shad roe, the event's real draw. A sought-after delicacy in more metropolitan places, shad roe has a storied reputation that brings certain vivid images to mind: the mid-century *New Yorker* writer Joseph Mitchell (from nearby Fairmont) reporting from the Fulton Fish Market over a shad-roe omelet; Cole Porter, musing on love and procreation, "Why ask if shad do it? Waiter, bring me shad roe"; and wealthy nineteenth-century Charlestonians, who breakfasted on roe with grits on fine china.

A delicate incision down the female shad's stomach liberates a pair of surprisingly large vaguely orange lobes, redolent of lungs. Connected by a bloody membrane, each pouch contains about 300,000 eggs, and they are most commonly poached or sautéed intact. In season, you can get shad roe at New York's Grand Central Oyster Bar, with bacon and a broiled tomato. Hominy Grill in Charleston sautés roe in butter and serves it with bacon, mushrooms, asparagus, lemon, garlic, and Tabasco, and at Atlanta's Empire State South, it's cured and plated with butter and sliced radishes.

Leonard explained the local recipe between industry complaints— about prices and regulation mostly—while stirring pounds of roe, gently sizzling in bacon grease donated by a local church. He added sage, thyme, shallot, and green onions, salt and pepper, and then poured in beaten hen eggs to give the roe texture and body. The result resembled a sandy mix of scrambled eggs and couscous, with a flavor that's difficult to describe. I removed myself from the bustle of diners to try and parse its elusive notes of smoke, liver, dirt, and brine. Earl Brown, witnessing my puzzled chewing, laughed and said, "That's caviar, man. Until I moved to New York, I had no idea I'd been eating caviar my entire life."

* * *

I MIGRATED BETWEEN picnic tables, where old friends bantered, comparing memories of past shad fries, fishing triumphs, and the rising prices of soda. I sat down next to Earl, who told me he hasn't missed Blue Monday in forty-three years. He had a low, booming voice and wore a gold shad medallion around his neck. Like many

East Arcadians during the Great Migration and the generation following, he moved north to make a living. "When I first got up there," he said, "I lost me a job for not showing up the day after Easter. I thought they got the day off up there too."

For Earl, before he returned home to retire, the shad fry was a time to reconnect with family. Now he and his friends, Jesse Blanks, a bail bondsman, and Jerry Graham, who came home twenty years ago, after retiring from the New York Transit Authority, provide financial support for the fry. When I asked them about the meaning of Blue Monday, they related the popular local belief that the tradition dates back to slaves on Cape Fear River plantations getting the day off after Easter, and taking that time to feast. Their account might be apocryphal, but it sounds plausible enough. The massive herring, shad, and mullet fisheries that once were common across the state from colonial times to the Civil War relied on a black workforce, both free and enslaved. This was highly skilled labor that involved piloting ships through the coast's notoriously treacherous shoals; dredging canals and seine runs, which required black divers to tamp explosives into thousand-year-old cypress roots; and wielding hand-woven nets, up to a mile-and-a-half long and brimming with tons of fish.

The degree of specialization and the comparatively lax oversight required by such labor, which often took place at night on the water, led many slave-holders to forgo coercive measures for rewards and incentives: wages, fishing allowances, and days off. For slaves on the Lloyd and Black Rock plantations, shad also would have supplemented their diet—and they likely engaged in illicit trade, using the fish to garner fatback, money, and other supplies. Certainly, the sudden influx of fresh meat, as winter pantries ran low, would have been more than welcome.

"It was a time of celebration, of spring coming," said Perry Dixon, the former mayor of the adjoining town of Sandyfield. He grew up farming in fields by the river and recalled the respite of fresh shad after winters of salted herring. They're used to celebrating holidays late, he added. Segregation-era East Arcadians observed the Fourth of July on the sixth on nearby Lake Waccamaw, after white revelers had cleared out.

Still, the story of Blue Monday is disputed. A number of groups in East Arcadia claim the shad fry tradition as their own, in spite of the state's recognition of one version. Later that afternoon, I checked out a competing Blue Monday celebration, where families in neon green T-shirts ate shad, roe, pepper-vinegar barbecue, and goat—pit-roasted, with salt, pepper, and thyme—in a dappled grove of unrestrained live oaks, a few minutes' drive from the lock and dam. In fact, practically everyone I spoke with in East Arcadia seemed to be the only one who knew what he or she was talking about.

I was surprised to find so much variation and controversy in a local tradition, but I've come to understand that these kinds of permutations are myriad in the region—and that the mild contention reflects a murkiness derived from the era of slavery. "These small communities look unified to outsiders, but cross a creek, and you'll find completely different histories, and differences of opinion that have persisted for centuries," said David Cecelski, author of *The Waterman's Song*, which details the region's porous racial boundaries. This was true for the isolated societies that sprouted along the region's remote waterways—mixed descendants of freed and runaway slaves, Indian survivors of the Tuscarora War, and poor whites who clung as dearly to their independence as they did the river for sustenance—and for former maritime slaves. All of these groups made up the population of East Arcadia in the nineteenth century, and their influences are still visible there today.

As Blue Monday drew to a close, Perry Dixon took me to the site of the former Lloyd Plantation, a shaded bend, where Highway 11 spans the water. The river barges, whose blaring horns many older locals recall hearing at night—with names like Tom Sawyer, Huck Finn, and Rebel—have gone the way of the once-vibrant fisheries. The lock and dam would have been blown up years ago if it didn't provide drinking water to Wilmington. But East Arcadians continue to rely on the river, for sustenance and for sense of self, and to gather, every Blue Monday, to sacramentally taste their Cape Fear origins.

A North Carolina native, JOHN McELWEE works in film and television development. He previously edited fiction at the *New Yorker*, and worked at a London-based literary agency. McElwee's work has appeared on newyorker.com and in the *Oxford American*—in collaboration with the photographer Chris Fowler, who contributed research and interviews to this piece.

Raising Goats to their Rightful Place

※ TOM RANKIN ※

WE RAISE GOATS. And to be more specific, Jill and I raise meat goats. I get asked from time to time—often at a refined gathering or a museum opening—something along the lines of "Do you all make cheese?" No, I always reply, adding that we barely have time to feed our herd in the busy mornings much less find time for daily milking. "They are meat goats," I add. The reaction is akin to what I imagine you see when you reveal a very, very serious diagnosis: a concerned, furrowed brow, a look of confused incredulity, a face at a loss for words.

Goats unquestionably provide the most popular meat worldwide and have always impressed me with their relative self-sufficiency. That's not to say they don't need care and animal husbandry, but compared to other mammals they get along quite well without requiring too much attention. As independent as they seem, goats, too, can fall ill with the best of any farm animal, need help birthing, or repeatedly get themselves caught in a fence they can't wiggle free from. But relative to the creatures moving around us day to day they are a self-reliant group, admirable in many ways.

Goats populate both the New and Old Testaments in abundance. The most notable reference is in Matthew, Chapter 25: ". . . he shall separate them one from another, as a shepherd divideth his sheep from the goats."[1] And from there, "And he shall set the sheep on his

---

1. Matthew Chapter 25: "And before him shall be gathered all nations: and he shall separate them one from another, as a shepherd divideth [his] sheep from the goats: (33) And he shall set the sheep on his right hand, but the goats on the left."

right hand, but the goats on the left." It is this verse that so clearly outlines an old world hierarchy as those "on the right" are advised to "inherit the kingdom prepared for you from the foundation of the world." Sometimes referred to as the "Parable of the Sheep," we learn that those on the right (the sheep, the redeemed) are eternally saved while those on the left (the goats, the lost) are forever damned. What do I make of such on the morning watch, on the daily feeding, as I trim hooves of our modest herd?

Might there be something noble about raising an animal that the Bible uses as the symbol of the lost, the unredeemed? Over the years the largest buyers of our goats have been new immigrant communities, Spanish-speakers to whom goat meat is a favorite, east and west Africans, and folks from Asia. To be sure, there's been a gradual shift in the American palate, with more and more farmers markets and new cuisine restaurants featuring goat meat. But the pace of change is slow, with lamb far more popular than the more common goat meat.

Recently I took two goats to Chaudhry Halal Meats for processing. I loaded two of our female boer goats—one white and one brown, both around a year old—into the back of my Toyota Tacoma for the drive from Hillsborough to Siler City. Wasim Chaudhry, one of Abdul and Shamim's three children, met me in the office area. Wasim is a UNC–Wilmington graduate, and the last time I was there he was heading to the coast to fish. He asked if I wanted to sell either goat, or have them processed. I paused for a minute, having not considered an outright sale. My plan to stock the freezer with homegrown meat won out, and I told him I wanted to leave them for processing. He immediately directed me to drive around back to meet a plant worker who would help me unload them. Grabbing first one and then the other by a leg, we moved the goats from the truck to a holding pen. A strictly Halal processing facility, Chaudhry employs over twenty people of diverse backgrounds and ethnicities, all working in the pork-free plant where each animal is ritually blessed before a major artery is severed for proper bleeding. Cows, sheep, and goats keep Chaudhry running at full capacity, with a long wait for anyone who wants cows slaughtered. For many years Chaudhry has processed all of Whole Foods grass-fed beef for North Carolina and Virginia—cows from Baldwin Family Farms in Yanceyville—and there is little room in the calendar for any other beef processing at this point.

I returned to the office where Wasim and I stood at the counter and started filling out the processing directions. The office walls are covered with wallpaper depicting early American scenes of a livery, of horses, of what looks to be an old house or inn, and of an early steam engine. The nostalgic images provide on incongruous back-drop for the Arabic-lettered tapestries and certificates of appreciation to Abdul Chaudhry from such organizations as "American's Registry of Outstanding Professionals," and the faded aerial photograph of the plant we are standing in.

"How do you want your shoulders?" Wasim asked. Sliced into steaks, I said, with a slight rise at the end suggesting I was not certain of the answer. "How thick?" he asked. How about a half inch, I de-cided quickly. "You sure you wouldn't like them three-quarters-inch thick?" I told him that I'd like two shoulders left whole for putting on my smoker. "Which goat—or does it matter?" he queried. "What size packages you want your ground meat in?" and on and on the ques-tions came. "Now, the loin chops. How thick should those be?" We moved over the whole body of a goat, all of the anatomy as under-stood by a meat cutter until I'd answered all the necessary questions, documented all the processing instructions. As Wasim was walking away to file the paperwork he turned and asked, "What about the heart and liver?" Yes, I said, I want them. "Is it okay to put them in one package?" Sure, why not, I said. The truth, which I didn't say, was that I planned to give my friend George the organs to use for bait in his coyote traps.

❋   ❋   ❋

I RETURNED TO pick up the meat several days later. Abdul Chaudhry was the only one in the office. He asked me to wait for a few minutes while he went outside to try to catch a goat that had escaped from his adjacent pasture. He returned, sweaty and tired, saying that it had gone into the woods and he'd catch it later. I offered to help but he declined.

After I'd loaded my meat in the cooler and paid my processing bill, I asked Abdul Chaudhry what in the world we were to make of Donald Trump. I knew full well where I was steering us, with Mr. Chaudhry a devout Muslim and Trump having slandered the faith in ways too numerous to catalog. Chaudhry said that Trump was crazy and then very calmly said, "None of my friends will be voting for him." It was reassuring the way he said it, such confidence in the best of our collective character. An immigrant from Pakistan who has built a multimillion-dollar business in the Piedmont of North Carolina, he didn't seem to see Trump as a threat.

Driving home with a cooler full of goat meat of the highest quality, I couldn't help but wonder why the goat gets such bad treatment in the Bible and in the popular American imagination. We call the player that drops the pass or strikes out in ninth inning "the goat," perhaps an outgrowth of that animal damned forever and without redemption. Isn't it possible that the Bible got it all wrong when it comes to goats, that the Parable of Sheep is just a story, and not to be taken as anything else? "So the last shall be first, and the first last," also from Matthew, may well be the best way to understand the hierarchy of meat, of seeing the possible slow-cooked redemption of goats.

TOM RANKIN is Professor of the Practice of Art and Documentary, director of the MFA in Experimental and Documentary Arts at Duke University, and former director of the Center for Documentary Studies. A photographer and writer, Rankin has been published in numerous magazines and journals. His books include *Sacred Space: Photographs from the Mississippi Delta* and *One Place: Paul Kwilecki and Four Decades of Photographs from Decatur County, Georgia.* He and his wife, Jill McCorkle, live on a farm in northern Orange County, where they raise chickens, goats, and tomatoes.

AFTERWORD

The Big Book of
North Carolina Foodways

☀ MARCIE COHEN FERRIS ☀

THE IDEA WAS to create an atlas of North Carolina foodways.[1]

We *know* one is needed—a definitive volume on the history of the Tar Heel State's cuisine—the diverse voices, dishes, ideas, places, and themes that characterize our state's distinctive foodways. Although a highly industrialized state, North Carolina remains proud of its vital farms and agricultural food production. Within North Carolina's diverse food cultures lie the harsh dynamics of racism, sexism, class struggle, and ecological exploitation; yet the state also nurtures family, a strong connection to place, conviviality, creativity, and flavor. The historic interactions between North Carolinians and what they eat tells us much about how they both differ from and resemble the rest of the South. A big, damn book. Maybe it's sitting on your coffee table. Yep, that's right. We couldn't find it either. No one's done it. Here's why.

It's complicated. We tried, and we're not giving up. The *we* is a devoted group of University of North Carolina students and faculty who spent two semesters studying the state's food cultures.[2] Our

---

1. Elizabeth Engelhardt defines foodways as "the study of why we eat, what we eat, and what it means." Elizabeth S.D. Engelhardt, "Redrawing the Grocery: Practices and Methods for Studying Southern Food," in *The Larder: Food Studies Methods from the American South*, eds. John T. Edge, Elizabeth Engelhardt, and Ted Ownby (Athens: University of Georgia Press, 2013), 1.

2. See website, including blog and oral history projects: http://carolinacooks.web .unc.edu/original-research/

quest began in the classroom, then moved to our kitchen tables. We gathered books that spoke to us about North Carolina and its inherent sense of place. We toted them by the armload—favorite authors and methods, histories, books on the state's agriculture, geography, migration, the changing economy, WPA guides from the 1930s, cookbooks, and old gazetteers. We discussed. We made lists. We listened to Charles Kuralt's *North Carolina Is My Home*. We brought in people to talk to us—people who have eaten, cooked, farmed, fished, taught, written, and legislated. We drew big maps of the state and its well-known regions—the coast, Eastern Carolina, the Piedmont, Western Carolina—positioning images of bright orange Snyder's-Lance ToastChee (Nabs) and sweet potato queens in their appropriate locations. We made more lists.

We bandied about terms like globalism, brand, narratives, contested borders, environmental degradation, malnourishment, industrialization, urbanization, and Calabashization (not a word, but a term I made up, meaning, "The marketing and branding of fried fish, Calabash-style."). Students recorded and transcribed oral histories, made videos with tinkly bluegrass soundtracks and cool digital presentations using the latest publishing and storytelling platforms. They explored topics like Texas Pete Hot Sauce (for a minute we thought we'd found the original Pete who inspired the lariat-tossing logo, but false alarm), Green's Lunch of Charlotte—famous for its tasty hot dogs—and the North Carolina State Fair's beloved Dairy Queen and rival ham biscuit booths.

As the semester came to a close, I thought long and hard about an atlas of North Carolina food cultures. Is it possible to capture the state's foodways in a single hidebound book published in a particular moment in time? How do we choose what to include—Cheerwine, pig farming, fish camps, peanuts, recipes, barbecue, sea rise, disenfranchisement, shuck beans, hunger, immigrant cooks, moonshine, sweet potatoes, craft beer? Surely telling the story of North Carolina's culinary cultures is a dynamic project that involves many voices and vibrant outcomes. But we *can* get at it, *can't we?* We eat it everyday. As a starting place, I'm taking a stab—fork, please—at a North Carolina food primer, a state culinary grammar, of sorts, inspired by the smart thinking of our food studies students. But, a few words about food and grammar and the people that have long pondered our state's food cultures.

I like to think about food as an expressive language of place. Not all North Carolinians speak the same *dialect* at the table—consider the state's venerated regions—yet citizens across the state share a common culinary language that allows them to understand and recognize one another. For example, if you're *from here*, you deeply respect the East/West Barbecue Divide and avoid saucing pork with tomatoes and vinegar willy-nilly. You know the difference between a Love Bun (traditionally served at a Moravian Lovefeast) and a Honey Bun (a Charlotte-made treat once sold from "dope wagons" that fueled hungry textile millworkers). You understand that Raleigh's famous Angus Barn steakhouse says as much about the mid-twentieth-century development of the Research Triangle Park technology corridor and the thousands who moved to the buckle of the Sunbelt as it does about the cache of aged beef.

North Carolina chefs, cooks, food writers, food entrepreneurs, folklorists, documentarians, filmmakers, food studies students, journalists, and back in the day, home economists, extension agents, and food columnists like Helen S. Moore who wrote weekly for the state's "Women's Pages," have examined and celebrated North Carolina's food and food cultures from the early twentieth century to the present. They, too, have grappled with defining the state's core foodways. In the 1930s and 1940s, food stories from North Carolina appeared in New Deal literary projects, including the Federal Writers Project's "Life Histories" that profiled food workers from lunch-counter waitresses to fishermen, the 1939 publication, *North Carolina: The WPA Guide to the Old North State,* with its period essay on "Eating and Drinking," and features on regional food, such as the tale of the upper Cape Fear, North Carolina "Chitterling Strut," collected for the "America Eats" project. Elizabeth Sparks—pen name Beth Tartan—was the award-winning food editor, home economist, and features writer for the *Winston-Salem Journal* from 1947 to 1991. A graduate of Old Salem College, she drew from her Moravian heritage to write her classic *North Carolina and Old Salem Cookery*.

From the 1940s to the 1960s, journalist Clementine Paddleford, food editor of the *New York Herald Tribune*, made an annual pilgrimage to the South to explore its food cultures. Evoking the mythologized romance of the "Lost Colony," Paddleford wrote about the "mother vineyard," the scuppernong vine of the Carolina Outer Banks, which she declared, "America's first grape."[3] Hundreds of North Carolina-authored cookbooks, both commercial and community-sponsored, were published throughout this era. A recent exhibit at the University of North Carolina's Wilson Library, "From Brunswick Stew to Barbecue: The Cookbook as Cultural Heritage," featured forty-nine cookbooks chosen from the more than nine hundred in the North Carolina Collection.[4]

In the second half of the twentieth century, culinary greats such as Bill and Moreton Neal, Edna Lewis, Ben and Karen Barker, Mildred Council, and Bill Smith transformed the North Carolina Piedmont into a hub of new Southern cuisine. *New York Times* food editor, Craig Claiborne, documented this burgeoning food scene. A long line of award-winning contemporary Southern chefs and restaurants are descended from these leaders and have created a legacy built on seasonality, simplicity, taste, imagination, and heritage. Farmers markets sprang to life in the last decades of the twentieth century, revitalizing the old curb markets of 1930s and 1940s. Ben Barker, an early chef supporter of the Carrboro Farmers Market, described its leaders as "a redoubtable group of hippies, back-to-the-land movement disciples, traditional farmers, and true visionaries."[5] Barker describes a symbiosis between the farmers and chefs who participated in the

3. Clementine Paddleford, "The Carolinas," in *How America Eats* (New York: Charles Scribner's Sons, 1960), 142.

4. http://blogs.lib.unc.edu/news/index.php/2015/06/cookbook-exhibit/

5. Ben Barker, "Chapel Hill Eats and a Chef Remembers," in *Cornbread Nation 5: The Best of Southern Food Writing*, ed. Fred Sauceman (Athens: University of Georgia Press, 2010), 171.

market. Chefs created a new demand for high quality, locally grown ingredients, and growers met that demand.

Today, a diverse culinary corps continues to create and chronicle North Carolina's evolving food cultures. Their wildly interdisciplinary work cuts a broad swath across North Carolina's cultural publications and media, farms, food-related businesses, home kitchens, museums, newspapers, organizations dedicated to food justice and sustainability, restaurants, and universities. Many of these voices appear in this volume.

Back to the idea of a *North Carolina Food Primer.* We remain inspired but humbled. North Carolina's foodways are constantly evolving, reflecting change over time in the state's people, culture(s), environment, geography, politics, and economies. Our students' voices capture this culinary moment. Kimber Thomas remarks, "North Carolina's food cultures are neither static nor easily defined. Investigating food exposes debates around citizenship, immigration, human and civil rights, and power. Who gets to eat where? Who is not eating? Who grows or cooks the food we consume? What does this tell us about inclusion, exclusion, and access in North Carolina?"

Absences are crucial when we analyze North Carolina foodways. The voices of women and racial and ethnic groups have been particularly silenced in both historic and contemporary narratives of the state's everyday eating places, processed and commercial foods, and sites of food tourism and leisure. Catherine Howell notes, "More often than not, the North Carolina food narrative that is the most important is the one that is missing."

The very foundation of North Carolina foodways reflects the state's rich racial, ethnic, and religious diversity. "The intersection of race and foodways goes far beyond a historical view of the South as white and black," writes Charlotte Fryar. "Instead, North Carolina's foodways are influenced by immigrant communities from Laos, Mexico, India, and many other countries, as well as the indigenous communities who have lived in the state the longest—the Lumbee, Cherokee, and Haliwa-Saponi tribes."

"Immigrant groups have made North Carolina food culture what it is today," Trista Reis Porter points out. "For example, the Greek-owned lunch counters (Ye Olde Waffle Shop in Chapel Hill) and hot dog stands (Dick's in Wilson), the Lebanese-founded Mount Olive Pickle Company, and the skilled Latino chefs, cooks, entrepreneurs, and farm laborers who are the backbone of the state's food economy."

Labor, industrialization, technological innovation, and a history of working class activism lie at the heart of North Carolina food cultures, as Jaycie Vos explains: "Many celebrated North Carolina foods are inextricably linked to the state's history of labor and industrialization. Pimento cheese and Cheerwine, for example, grew in popularity due to demand by textile mill workers who needed quick, cheap foods they could eat while at work."

In the years since my husband, Bill, and I first moved to North Carolina, we have experienced this beautiful state, its rich culture, its people, and even today's contested politics through memorable moments and conversations at the table. We have eaten North Carolina food prepared by North Carolinians of many races and ethnicities from the coast, Eastern Carolina, the Piedmont, and the mountains. We have witnessed an evolving state as we savor both old school fried croaker and steaming bowls of North Carolina-style ramen. Charlotte Fryar captured one more quintessential rule of North Carolina's cuisine: "There is no unified idea of North Carolina foodways that does not separate the state into its different regions."

Go out and taste this state, and when you do, hold onto those stories. *The Big Book of North Carolina Foodways* is yet to come.

MARCIE COHEN FERRIS is a professor of American Studies at the University of North Carolina at Chapel Hill. She is the author of *Matzoh Ball Gumbo: Culinary Tales of the Jewish South* and, most recently, the award-winning *The Edible South: The Power of Food and the Making of an American Region*. Ferris also serves as an editor for *Southern Cultures*, a quarterly journal sponsored by UNC's Center for the Study of the American South.

☀ ABOUT THE EDITOR ☀

PHOTO BY MIRIAM BERKLEY

RANDALL KENAN is professor of English at the University of North Carolina at Chapel Hill, as well as an award-winning novelist, journalist, and food writer. He has written about food for a variety of publications, most notably a profile of culinary food historian Michael Twitty for *Garden & Gun*. He also teaches a course on Food Writing at UNC.

His books include *Visitation of the Spirits, Let the Dead Bury Their Dead,* and *The Fire This Time.* He has received numerous awards and honors, including the North Carolina Award for Literature in 2005, and was elected to the Fellowship of Southern Writers in 2007. He also is the recipient of the John Dos Passos Prize and the Rome Prize of the American Academy or Arts and Letters.

A native of Duplin County, Mr. Kenan now lives and pursues his culinary interests in Hillsborough, North Carolina.

☀ EPIGRAPH BIOGRAPHY NOTE ☀

"Home in Mind," which appears as the epigraph to *The Carolina Table*, is the work of Sheila Smith McKoy. She is the editor of both volumes of *The Elizabeth Keckley Reader* (Eno Publishers), and is a poet, prosaist, and literary critic. A native North Carolinian and a long-time professor at North Carolina State University, Smith McKoy is now chair of the English Department at Kennesaw State University. She is also the author of *When Whites Riot: Writing Race and Violence in American and South African Cultures*, which received critical acclaim in the U.S. and in Africa.

✳ RECIPE INDEX ✳

☀ PERMISSIONS & ACKNOWLEDGMENTS ☀

Lee Smith's story "The Recipe Box" is from *Dimestore* ©2016 by Lee Smith. Reprinted by permission of Algonquin Books of Chapel Hill. All rights reserved.

John McElwee's "Blue Monday" is adapted from his story by the same name that originally was published in *The Oxford American* (Fall 2014).

Heather Newton's story "Lessons in Table Manners" is adapted from a blog post she published on bookclubgirl.com.

Steven Petrow's story "The Pies That Bind" is adapted from a story that first appeared in the *New York Times* (December 20, 2013).

Marianne Gingher's "Pie Love You, Cake Do Without You" is adapted from a piece that was originally published in *Southern Cultures* (Spring 2015).

Daniel Wallace's essay "The Mesopotamia of Pork" is adapted from his story that originally appeared in the October 2014 issue of *Our State* magazine.

The 27 Views Series

27 *Views of Hillsborough: A Southern Town in Prose & Poetry*
Introduction by Michael Malone
$15.95
ISBN 978-0-9820771-2-2

27 *Views of Chapel Hill: A Southern University Town
in Prose & Poetry*
Introduction by Daniel Wallace
$16.50
ISBN 978-0-9820771-9-1

27 *Views of Asheville: A Southern Mountain Town
in Prose & Poetry*
Introduction by Rob Neufeld
$15.95
ISBN 978-0-9832475-1-7

27 *Views of Durham: The Bull City in Prose & Poetry*
Introduction by Steve Schewel
$15.95
ISBN 978-0-9832475-3-1

27 Views of Raleigh: The City of Oaks in Prose & Poetry
Introduction by Wilton Barnhardt
$15.95
ISBN 978-0-9832475-5-5

_____

27 Views of Charlotte: The Queen City in Prose & Poetry
Introduction by Jack Claiborne
$14.95
ISBN 978-0-9832475-9-3

_____

27 Views of Greensboro: The Gate City in Prose & Poetry
Introduction by Marianne Gingher
$15.95
ISBN 978-0-9896092-1-0

_____

27 Views of Wilmington: The Port City in Prose & Poetry
Introduction by Celia Rivenbark
$15.95
ISBN 978-0-9896092-3-4

_____

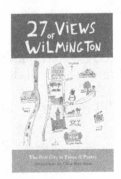

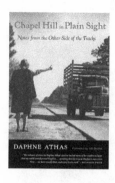

Chapel Hill in Plain Sight:
Notes from the Other Side of the Tracks
by Daphne Athas
$16.95
ISBN 978-0-9820771-3-9

_____

Undaunted Heart:
The True Story of a Southern Belle and a Union General
by Suzy Barile
$16.95
ISBN 978-0-9820771-1-5

_____

Behind the Scenes:
Thirty Years a Slave, and Four Years in the White House
by Elizabeth Keckley
Introduction by Dolen Perkins-Valdez
$10.00
ISBN 978-0-9896092-7-2

_____

The Elizabeth Keckley Reader, Vol. 1
Edited by Sheila Smith McKoy
$15.95
ISBN 978-0-9896092-5-8

Eno Publishers   www.enopublishers.org